Reclaiming Offender Accountability: Intermediate Sanctions for Probation and Parole Violators

A Project of the
American Correctional Association's 1990-1992
Committee on Probation, Parole, and Supervised Release

Edited by Edward E. Rhine

American Correctional Association 1990-1992
Committee on Probation, Parole, and Supervised Release

Perry M. Johnson, President
James A. Gondles, Jr., Executive Director
Patricia L. Poupore, Director of Communications and Publications
Elizabeth Watts, Publications Managing Editor
Marianna Nunan, Project Editor
Jennifer A. Nichols, Production Editor
Ann M. Tontodonato, Cover Design

ISBN 0-929310-59-4

Printed in the United States of America by BookCrafters, Fredricksburg, Va.

This publication may be ordered from:
American Correctional Association
8025 Laurel Lakes Court
Laurel, MD 20707-5075
1-800-825-BOOK

Contents

Foreword

Reclaiming Offender Accountability: Intermediate Sanctions for Probation and Parole Violators is the work of the American Correctional Association's Committee on Probation, Parole, and Supervised Release. The chapters in this monograph provide a wealth of information on how intermediate sanctions are used in federal, state, and county probation and parole systems. They offer insight to the successes and failures of implementing and using a variety of intermediate sanctions in several different jurisdictions.

Administrators interested in exploring the use of intermediate sanctions for probation and parole violators or those refining programs already in place will find this monograph useful and practical. Administrators can save time, money, and effort by learning from the experiences of professionals who have worked through the intricacies involved in developing and using intermediate sanctions programs.

The age of intermediate sanctions for probation and parole is here. It is time to explore how intermediate sanctions can play a part in solving the crowding crisis. In this monograph, ACA's committee of prominent professionals and program experts share their experiences with you. It is with great thanks that we recognize their contributions.

James A. Gondles, Jr.
Executive Director
American Correctional Association

Preface

There are more than one million offenders in U.S. prisons and jails. Prisons across the country are finding that they do not have adequate bed space and other resources for the large numbers of offenders flowing into their systems. A significant number of offenders crowd jails as they wait for bed space in prisons. In 1991, more than 12,000 state inmates were being held in local jails or other facilities because of crowding in state institutions ("Prisons in 1991," *BJS Bulletin* [May 1992]). It is not surprising, then, to find that the prison population crisis is an area of concern for corrections and criminal justice officials, legislators, researchers, and others.

The prison population consists of offenders who are sentenced directly from the courts after conviction as well as those who have had their parole or probation revoked. It is in this latter area of probation and parole where we consistently find the greatest number of offenders. During 1990, the U.S. probation population increased 5.9 percent to 2.67 million, and parole increased 16.3 percent to 530,000 ("Probation and Parole 1990," *BJS Bulletin* [November 1991]). Indeed, the growth in probation and parole has been faster than in prisons and jails. Over the past decade, the area of probation and parole grew 139 percent, while prison and jail population growth increased 128 percent.

The fact that a large number of offenders in the criminal justice system are on parole or probation, coupled with the fact that in some states roughly two-thirds of prison admissions result from parole and probation revocations, leads to the obvious conclusion that revocation policies have significant impact on prison population. This monograph provides useful information concerning current activities relative to supervised release, parole and probation revocation policies, and procedures and implementation of program strategies to include intermediate sanctions. The sweeping focus includes "what is happening" and the rationale for it in various locations—national, state, and county perspectives for the United States and Canada.

The Committee on Probation, Parole, and Supervised Release, under the leadership of Edward E. Rhine, who served as its chairperson, has performed an outstanding service to the field. As a service organization and because knowledge is the prelude to progress and improvement, the American Correctional Association prides itself on being an important resource for the field. This committee has made a significant contribution to this effort. I am tremendously indebted to the professionals who served on this committee as well as those whose materials are included in this publication.

The Honorable Helen G. Corrothers
ACA Past President

Introduction

By Lloyd G. Rupp

Reclaiming Offender Accountability: Intermediate Sanctions for Probation and Parole Violators was undertaken by the American Correctional Association's Committee on Probation, Parole, and Supervised Release. Its purpose is to establish a benchmark with respect to the state-of-the-art in probation and parole as we come to the close of the twentieth century and begin to consider the issues, challenges, and possibilities for criminal justice practitioners in the twenty-first century.

The work is by no means an attempt to deal with all the issues of intermediate sanctions, absconding, probation and parole violations, or the many other issues facing the judiciary, law enforcement, probation, parole, community control, or corrections practitioners within the criminal justice continua. It is, however, reflective of the history and development of the agencies that have struggled to provide North American society with a modicum of social safety coupled with a humane system of dealing with the increasing numbers of persons who, for whatever reasons, have not been able to accommodate their behavior to society's norms as expressed in the law.

If nothing else, this society has distinguished itself by the sheer numbers of individuals it has selectively incarcerated and socially controlled in the twentieth century. Just a glance at Bureau of Justice Statistics reports from the past few years makes it clear that we, as a nation, have placed more people under the control of our criminal justice system than any other society. According to the Bureau of Justice Statistics (1991), the number of people on probation increased by 36 percent and those on parole increased by 77 percent between 1985 and 1990. Correctional populations rose by 52.8 percent during that same period.

Intermediate Sanctions—Their Place in Corrections

This compilation of articles begins with Parent's thought-provoking look at structuring violation and absconding policies. He chronicles the often confusing and contradictory responses to data within the same agency. He also chronicles the dramatic increase in parole revocations and the profound effect they have had on prison crowding and the increased cost of construction and administration that ensued. The experience of California, Texas, Minnesota, Oregon, and others are exemplary of the national problem. Parent's view of the "passive approach" to absconders will surprise no one who has been in the field the past few decades, and he raises an interesting and insightful parallel between absconding and inactive caseloads. Parent offers a helpful paradigm of policy objectives (deterrence, rehabilitation, just punishment, due process, and system management) with respect to sanctioning violators.

Parent explores some innovative policies for responding to violations and absconding. These policies run the gamut from agency administrative initiatives to statutory responses.

In "Handling Violations of Probation and Supervised Release at the Federal Level," Burress examines federal, state, and local strategies for responding to violations by offenders under community supervision. Burress begins his chapter with a detailed look at the federal response to violations of probation and supervised release.

He presents a useful discussion of the theoretical considerations with respect to sanctioning violations of probation and supervised release. The adoption of a revocation policy that provides for "broad grades of violations" ultimately meets the proportionality rule, which seems consistent with the commission's charter to provide "certainty and fairness" in sentencing.

Turning to the issues of intermediate sanctions for federal parole violators, Clay and Grinner make the case for intermediate sanctions. The authors review the 1988 community control project in the Southern District of Florida and Central California and intensive supervision project in Hyattsville, Maryland. Reviewing the community sanctions evaluation project, the authors note how the parameters for these technical violators targeted substance abusers and avoided the "net widening" phenomenon.

Turning to the most recent and creative expansion of intermediate sanctions, the authors review the federal parole violator sanctions center. A joint project of the U.S. Parole Commission, Federal Probation, and the Federal Bureau of Prisons (BOP), the parole violator sanctions centers will initially be established in the Washington, D.C., area and operated in BOP-funded community correction centers.

In the next chapter, the New York State Division of Parole's Office of Policy Analysis and Information presents an overview of the parole revocation process in New York State. To manage the state's large parole population, a system of differential supervision has been instituted. A variety of intermediate sanctions are employed, including residential transient facilities, electronic monitoring, a novel jail-based high-impact incarceration program (HIIP), and special substance abuse treatment provisions. Alternatives to reincarceration include transitional facilities; high-impact incarceration programs; treatment alternatives to street crime; the assigned council alternative program, which includes an alternative to reincarceration unit; and electronic monitoring through VOREC VOICENET.

Next, Herman provides a concise history of Missouri's response to technical violators. He discusses how rapid and large growth in parole and probation populations called for a well-coordinated response by all divisions of the Missouri Department of Corrections (DOC). The DOC's development of the Kansas City Recycling Center, Tipton Treatment Center, St. Louis Community Release Center, and the Mineral Area Treatment Centers demonstrates a highly coordinated effort to solve the pressures on overburdened correctional facilities. Herman shows how the development of primary probation/parole supervision, intensive supervision, house arrest, electronic monitoring programs, residential treatment facilities, and shock probation work in combination to provide the "balance of control, structure, treatment, and intervention" that will ensure the taxpayers of Missouri that they are getting the most cost-effective and productive effort from the DOC.

In "The Parole Violations Process in Georgia," Prevost, Rhine, and Jackson provide a well-documented review of innovative violations/revocation policy in response to Georgia's prison crowding. In the 1980s the Georgia State Board of

Pardons and Parole, in addition to its traditional roles of granting clemency and providing community supervision for offenders, assumed primary responsibility for prison population control. Because revocation and return of a parolee to prison required the board to release an inmate who was currently confined, the board developed informal and formal sanctions, including a continuum of intermediate sanctions, to precede outright revocation and reincarceration. Indicative of the board's creativity was the adoption of the "back end" program of electronic monitoring, the establishment of a parole violators' unit in a joint effort with the Department of Corrections, and the development of a NIJ-sponsored task group.

Next, Grubbs chronicles the growth trends in Mississippi's prison, probation, and parole populations. The Mississippi DOC is sensitive to and works with circuit court judges who have their individual concerns (drugs, restitution, etc.) and differences in probation policies among their several jurisdictions. In recognition of the role drugs play in absconding and noncompliance, the department responded with regional drug identification officers who are trained to provide appropriate assessment, monitor treatment programs, and maintain close community resource contacts. Developing appropriate community-based treatment programs and meaningful drug testing is emphasized.

In "Probation and Parole and the Use of Intermediate Sanctions in Ontario, Canada," Page outlines practices in Ontario, the most populous province in Canada. The Canadian system does not suffer from the pressure of prison and jail crowding found in the United States. The term "intermediate sanctions" is not widely used among corrections professionals in Ontario, and such sanctions are not used when dealing with probation and parole revocations. Yet, there is a process called "temporary absence" (e.g., supervised release for employment, education, medical, or compassionate conditions), and there are familiar programs like intensive supervision, shock incarceration, weekend sentences, restitution, and community service that have been used for some time. Electronic monitoring, urinalysis, boot camps, and attendance centers are being considered. There are clearly philosophical differences between the Canadian criminal justice system and that of the United States; however, the steady increase in crime rates, particularly for violent crimes, in Canada may lead to more serious interest in the use of intermediate sanctions.

Next, Stroker describes how the South Carolina Department of Probation, Parole and Pardon Services developed a guiding philosophy on handling violations committed while under community supervision and a set of interrelated expectations, guidelines, procedures, and policy that would increase the consistency of their responses to violations and take into account both the risk for the individual to the community and the severity of the violation committed. He demonstrates the benefits of having administrative hearing officers use clear violations guidelines and expanded community control options. He emphasizes the "hard-dollar" savings that can be gained from community-based offender control. Indeed, the issue of hard-dollar savings through the use of community control may well become the prevailing argument under the reality of budgetary constraints.

In "Responding to Probation Violators: The Case of the Cook County Adult Probation Department," Lurigio, Robinson, and Klosak delineate the legislative and administrative history of Cook County, Illinois, probation and parole systems in the context of concurrent national trends. They demonstrate how in 1978 changes in laws providing determinate sentencing structure and class X felony provisions led to a forced-release program in 1980, which sent 10,000 inmates out into the community under accelerated release. When the court invalidated the practice in 1983, populations in prisons and jails increased dramatically. The authors note that the probation population has outpaced the prison, jail, or parole populations. They present significant data on felony probation and the effect of high-risk offender populations, increased caseloads, higher recidivism rates, and concomitant budget cuts.

In "The Expanded Use of Intermediate Sanctions in Morris County, New Jersey," Del Preore looks at the trends on the county level and at "dispositional enforcement" in a community-based system. He shows us that Morris County judges are using alternative intermediate sanctions in response to serious jail crowding. The coordination and cooperation of the Sheriff's Office, County Probation Services, and the courts and municipalities demonstrate innovative responses at the community level. Sanctions that include community service, jail tours, house curfew, electronic monitoring, high-intensity probation, and the Sheriff's Labor Assistance Program characterize this responsive program. Del Preore notes that Morris County has moved to centralize court enforcement by using the same superior court judge to ensure consistent sentencing policy and to streamline sentencing practices. The results of this effort pose a model for the counties where resources are scarce and citizens demand the maximum in community safety for the minimum dollar expended.

In the final chapter, "Intermediate Sanctions and Violations Policy in Probation and Parole: Prescriptions for the 1990s," Rhine and Humphries provide the reader with some thought-provoking conclusions. Reciting the litany of population explosions in probation, parole, and confinement, the authors begin by pointing out that although intermediate sanctions are a response to the challenge of crowded jails and prisons, inconsistent policy, uneven responses, and incoherent policy framework lead to staff confusion, increased costs, and less effective supervision.

The authors review the National Institute of Corrections model probation/parole classification and case management project of the 1980s. They point out that the four-point model, instrument-based risk and needs assessment, adoption of client management classification for case planning, and use of a management information system are most notable in their affect on risk and needs assessments as a fundamental tool to enhance supervision case management. What is often overlooked, however, is the link between supervision case management and responses to probation and parole violators. According to the authors, the agency's philosophy of supervision will determine the goals and parameters, and the blend and balance must be unique to each agency. The agency, itself, must operate in the realm of its constituent environment, and its policies will be shaped by the tensions within it.

Turning to the issue of technical violations, the authors present data from two studies that point to the efficacy of taking a hard look at which offenders are violating and why. They argue that a "differential response" makes good sense if one's goal is to ensure personal accountability and ameliorative intervention.

They call for a clear definition of the rationale for and use of intermediate sanctions. They say that both probation and parole will profit from the same judicious use of intermediate sanctions and that "it is essential that judges, parole boards, and agency decision makers with responsibility for supervision ensure that field staff understand the fit between responses to violations and the appropriate use of intermediate sanctions."

Special Concerns

In reviewing this monograph of intermediate sanctions and violations policies, there are some issues that appear to warrant additional comment.

In many states there has been a discernable, if not dramatic, movement from what has been termed the "social work model" to heavy emphasis in "surveillance" activities designed to catch clients in technical violation or recurrent criminality and "get them off the streets before they cause more trouble." This has been called a law enforcement or community control model. The result, as Parent points out, has been an increase in the number of people behind bars and an exacerbation of prison crowding. Recognizing the problematic nature of drug-addicted offenders who have driven our criminal justice system for the past several decades, there has been increased pressure to make an immediate effort to get them off the street and into some form of more restricted social control or into some sort of treatment. California, for instance, has developed a unique form of institution that is specifically designed for those individuals who were headed back into prison, mostly by virtue of continued drug abuse. These institutions are specially designed to make a positive intervention in the lives of such offenders using a combination of incarceration, work programs, education, and substance abuse programming. Such institutions, while not inexpensive, offer a viable alternative to lengthy reincarceration.

As community control systems develop, we may well see a gradual synthesis of this social work/law enforcement dichotomy. It may be too early to tell the exact implications of this developmental process. The recent trends toward intermediate sanctions chronicled in this monograph will undoubtedly play a significant role in the ensuing shape of the model in the twenty-first century. It does seem clear that the probation and parole officer of the twenty-first century will be required to provide an even higher level of professional skill and judgment than heretofore required.

A proposed working definition of sanctions is: A penalty, specified or in the form of moral pressure, that acts to ensure compliance or conformity. Compulsory substance abuse treatment, for instance, falls within that definition. Indeed, any restriction or deprivation of a person's freedom of choice with respect to time and place is, in some sense, a sanction. Some intermediate sanctions are rightly viewed as appropriate punishment for miscreant behavior. Shock incarceration—boot camps run by correctional staff—however well-intended by those who design them, are viewed by the general public as certain form of punishment.

However, given the fact that our criminal justice system today is drug-ridden and drug-driven, it is important to understand that field personnel are often fighting a life-and-death battle for their offenders' sobriety, knowing that if the offenders' treatment can be facilitated, their criminal behavior will, in many cases, be curtailed, if not stopped. If such intervention is not successful, it is almost certain the continued drug use will end in the death of the user, or of someone else. For field practitioners, then, it may not be useful to present substance abuse treatment as a sanction.

Likewise, urinalysis is mildly intrusive. It also helps keep addicts straight. Day treatment facilities can provide vital support to at-risk offenders. Additional reporting sessions can provide needed counseling for offenders who are having difficulty adjusting to the real world. Community service can establish solid feelings of self-worth and accomplishment. Work training can lay a foundation for crime-free living.

Intensive supervision is a form of case management that establishes the possibility of developing a mentoring relationship between a parole or probation officer and the offender. It is more than monitoring an offender's activities to "catch him or her doing bad."

The point is that, with respect to intermediate sanctions, the messages we send can make all the difference between effective supervision and setting offenders up for failure. In our rush to sell intermediate sanctions to our constituents it would seem important to make sure we are not defeating the fundamental mission of the agency: to restore the offender to the community as a law abiding, functional, tax-paying citizen.

Several who have shared their insights and experience in the pages of this book have argued that intermediate sanctions represent a return to a more rational system of case management. The idea that such responses by probation and parole agencies are a punitive or sanctioning device needs to be explored more fully in terms of its implications on the program in general and on the offender in particular.

Another issue that warrants closer scrutiny is that of cost-effectiveness. As Rhine and Humphries have pointed out, there can be some serious consequences when agencies are not forthcoming as to the "up-front" expenses of establishing intermediate sanctions. The agency must carefully reckon the near-term costs, and these must be presented to the agencies' funding sources and the general public in a straightforward manner. In most cases, over the long haul, some positive cost-saving should be achieved.

The contributors of this monograph hope that it will stimulate agencies and their constituents to embrace the challenge of the twenty-first century with a renewed sense of optimism. Change is inevitable. Positive change is the product of sound reasoning, professional management, and innovative responses to the opportunity and challenges that come to us each day.

Reference

Bureau of Justice Statistics. 1991. Probation and parole in 1990. *BJS Bulletin* (November).

Chapter 1

Structuring Policies to Address Sanctions for Absconders and Violators

By Dale G. Parent

Recent research shows marked increases in the number of probation and parole violators. In some states, two-thirds of those admitted to prison are those who have had their probation or parole revoked, not newly sentenced offenders. In response, some states are developing new ways to handle violations that rely on swift and certain, but not severe, punishment and that use existing intermediate sanctions to match the severity of the punishment to the seriousness of the violation. Others are developing more effective ways to track, locate, apprehend, and, if necessary, extradite absconders. As prison crowding worsens, more states will be moved to rethink their traditional responses to violators.

Recently, the president of a statewide union representing probation and parole officers said it was becoming difficult to enforce conditions of supervision because revocation was a hollow threat. Testing showed drug use was rampant. Revocation procedures were slow and complicated. When violators had their probation or parole revoked and were imprisoned, they were released in a few days because of crowding and court-imposed capacity limits. The Department of Corrections (DOC) even furloughed some low-risk revokees held in jails awaiting transport to state facilities, thus by-passing prison altogether. Absconding rates were skyrocketing because offenders knew if they were caught they would not face long prison terms. Current practices, he believed, sent the wrong messages to offenders: the first few violations were freebies. When authorities finally pulled the trigger, offenders quickly saw they were shooting blanks.

A top correctional official in the same state said revocations were out of control and threatened to destroy the system. Revocation rates had tripled in the past ten years. Revocations, not new sentences, accounted for two-thirds of the state's prison admissions. Although some revoked offenders were released quickly to relieve crowding, most served substantial prison terms and contributed heavily to the crowding problem. The state had doubled its prison capacity in the past five years. Both the governor and the legislature balked at more funding for prison expansion because other constituents wanted those funds to go to education, roads, health care, and libraries.

These two officials in the same agency had starkly different views of the situation. According to the union president, the solution was to punish violators more severely to deter future violations—build more prisons, if necessary, so violators would not be released early. The DOC administrator's solution was to imprison fewer violators and return low-risk violators to community supervision even more quickly.

What's Happening with Revocations?

In 1990 a private consulting firm was retained by the National Institute of Justice (NIJ) to study trends in probation and parole revocation. Probation and parole officials in all fifty states were interviewed and available data were reviewed. The consultants then visited six jurisdictions to observe innovative programs in operation.

According to Bureau of Justice Statistics (BJS) (1991) census data, probation and parole populations increased dramatically in recent years. Between 1980 and 1988 probation populations grew 83 percent, from 1.2 million to 2.2 million, and parole populations grew 60 percent, from 225,827 to 362,192. During the same time, prison populations increased 77.6 percent. Admissions to probation during this time grew 96 percent, from 736,250 to 1,440,000. Between 1980 and 1987, parole admissions grew 92 percent, from 125,000 to 240,000.

Given the growth in probation and parole population, an increase in the number of probation and parole revocations would be expected, even if revocation rates were constant. However, in about one-third of the states, rates of revocation have also risen.

Several factors may contribute to the increase in probation and parole revocations:

1. The mission of community supervision has changed. During the 1980s administrators built political support for probation and parole by emphasizing that community supervision punished offenders and protected the public. Surveillance and control replaced treatment as the main goals of community supervision.
2. Control-oriented supervision strategies have improved the ability to detect violations. Most probation and parole agencies use risk-based screening and classification. Many have implemented intensive supervision, routine drug testing, and, to a lesser extent, electronic monitoring. These changes increase the odds that violations will be detected, even if the rate of violations is unchanged.
3. Different people are being recruited to work in probation and parole. Twenty years ago social work was the most common educational path for those pursuing careers in probation or parole. Today, the most common educational path is criminal justice studies—an academic field spawned in the 1960s to professionalize law enforcement. Today's recruits may be better equipped to understand issues of power and authority than they are to understand human behavior and how to change it.
4. Today's offenders may be different. Many in the field believe today's offenders are likely to be more involved with drugs, to have committed more serious crimes, to have longer prior-arrest records, and to have begun their criminal careers at younger ages than in the past. Others maintain that today's offenders are similar to those of the past, but that today's comprehensive conditions of supervision and use of

sophisticated techniques to detect violations have led to an increase in the number of violators detected.

5. New sentencing options increase the chance of violation. Judges with new sentencing options are more likely to impose multiple conditions of supervision, thereby increasing the odds that offenders will violate some conditions before completing supervision.

Because the number of offenders on probation and parole far exceeds the number in prisons, even small changes in revocation rates have big effects on prison admissions and populations. A five percentage point increase in revocation rates, coupled with a doubling of the probation and parole population as occurred during the past decade, can triple the number of offenders admitted to prisons as violators.

BJS prison admission data show that between 1982 and 1987 the number of offenders admitted to prisons following revocation of parole and other forms of conditional release (i.e., work release and furlough, but excluding probation) rose 113 percent, from 39,003 to 82,959. The proportion of these violators returned to prison without a new sentence (e.g., technical violators) rose from 51 percent to 61 percent. Parole violators and other supervised release violators as a percentage of total prison admissions increased from 16.9 percent to 24.4 percent.

Although the BJS reports do not provide trend data specifically on probation violators, it is generally agreed that the number of probationers who were revoked and imprisoned has risen significantly in recent years (BJS 1991).

In Oregon, more than 60 percent of prison admissions in 1988 were probation and parole violators (Parent et al., in press). Two-thirds of Texas' prison admissions were probation or parole violators. In Minnesota, 40 percent of prison admissions were probation or supervised release violators, nearly double the rate from a dozen years ago.

In California, the 1990 Blue Ribbon Commission on Prison Crowding found the following:

1. The number of parole revocations rose from fewer than 2,000 in 1978 to more than 34,000 in 1988.
2. The rate of parole revocation rose 350 percent during that time.
3. In 1988 more than half of California's prison admissions were parole violators.
4. The average offender whose parole had been revoked served more than one year in prison in 1988. Thus, parole violators alone occupied about 34,000 prison beds on an average day in 1988.

What's Happening with Absconders?

Little research has been done on absconders. In 1975 the Florida Parole and Probation Commission analyzed characteristics of absconders and found that absconders reflected the general population under supervision in terms of race, education, history of alcohol or drug use, number of prior arrests, prison commitments, prior revocations (probation or parole), juvenile record, and prior record of escape or absconding.

In the NIJ study, probation and parole officials indicated that the number and rate of absconding has risen in recent years. Typical absconders were described as low-risk property offenders who remained in the community after they absconded. Although their lifestyles might not be exemplary, most absconders were not arrested for new crimes while on absconder status, and hence, arguably may have posed little risk to the public.

In many states, sentences continue to run and can expire while offenders are on absconder status, preventing absconder caseloads from ballooning. However, some states toll time on the sentence when an absconder warrant is issued, allowing the number of absconders to grow.

Most states take a passive approach to absconders. They file an arrest warrant, place notice of the warrant on law enforcement information systems, and wait. If police arrest the absconder within the same jurisdiction, the probation or parole agency usually will take custody and commence revocation. If the offender is arrested in another state, the agency must decide whether to extradite the offender. In states that take a passive approach, the main function of the fugitive unit is to transport apprehended absconders. Their absconder policies are often similar to those used for offenders placed on inactive or administrative caseloads. One agency has an unwritten policy that if absconders remain arrest-free for five years, their sentences will be discharged; the agency follows this same policy for parolees on inactive supervision. An agency official said the main difference between inactive caseloads and absconders is that the latter are self-selected.

Policy Objectives of Sanctioning Violators

There are at least five policy objectives for sanctioning offenders who violate conditions of supervision: deterrence, rehabilitation, just punishment, due process, and system management.

Deterrence

Many of the probation and parole officials interviewed believe the threat of revocation and punishment deters future violations both by those sanctioned (specific deterrence) and by others on probation or parole (general deterrence). Conversely, they believe that offenders who think they will not be sanctioned are more likely to commit more violations. Thus, violations must be sanctioned to keep offenders on supervision, a necessary precondition to achieve any other supervision objective, such as treatment or restitution.

In theory, violations could be deterred by inflicting the following:

- severe punishment—as severity of sanctions increases, the number of violations should decline
- swift punishment—the number of violations should decline if the interval between the violation and the sanction is shortened
- certain punishment—the number of violations should decline if the probability of being sanctioned increases

In the past, agencies have tried to deter violations by adjusting the severity of sanctions, but they have done little in terms of changing sanctions' swiftness or establishing certainty. Relying mainly on severe sanctions to deter violations may conflict with other objectives. For example, a long prison term may be unduly harsh for a minor violation. Imprisoning violators may undercut other aims of the sentence, such as treatment or restitution. Officials often do not impose severe sanctions for an offender's first few violations, thus diminishing certainty and swiftness of sanctions. Furthermore, as prisons and jails become increasingly crowded, it becomes more and more problematic to impose severe sanctions on probation and parole violators.

Rehabilitation

Most offenders do not volunteer for treatment. Instead, they must be compelled to enter and continue in treatment. The threat of revocation, therefore, is a tool that gets reluctant offenders into treatment and keeps them there.

Just Punishment

Advocates of just punishment argue that the sanction imposed on violators should fit the seriousness of the violation. Minor violations should get modest sanctions, while major violations should get severe sanctions. For example, revoking probation and imprisoning an offender for five years for violating probation by committing a misdemeanor would not fit the seriousness of the violation because individuals convicted on misdemeanor charges face a maximum sentence of only thirty days in jail.

Due Process

Revocation policy also involves fundamental questions about due process rights. When revocation is used as a substitute for prosecution on new alleged crimes, the burden of proof is lowered from "beyond a reasonable doubt" to a "preponderance of evidence," and a far less rigorous administrative hearing procedure is substituted for trial court proceedings.

System Management

Revocation policy involves system management considerations, both for institutional and community corrections and for the broader criminal justice system. Prosecutors often prefer to revoke probationers and parolees who are charged with new crimes, particularly when the alleged new offense is minor or the evidence is too weak to prove the crime beyond a reasonable doubt.

Processing probation violators uses a lot of court resources. Probation officers who process violation paper work and appear for revocation hearings have less time to supervise offenders. Violators held for revocations contribute to jail crowding. Revocation policy has major implications for workloads and resources at all levels of criminal justice.

Innovative Policies for Responding to Violations

Several jurisdictions have developed innovative ways to handle offenders who violate probation or parole requirements or who abscond. Some were designed to deter by imposing swift and certain, but not necessarily severe, punishment on violators. Others make punishment for violators uniform and proportional to the seriousness of the violation. Many methods are not grounded in theory, but are responses to a crisis situation.

Administrative Review and Approval of Revocations

Oregon and Michigan require supervisors to review and approve revocation petitions using criteria designed to limit the numbers approved. The burden of going through this process, along with the prospect of a petition being rejected, may discourage some line officers from commencing the revocation process. Typically, these programs are aimed at reducing prison admissions and crowding.

Many probation and parole officers strongly resist supervisory review and approval of revocations. They maintain that it curtails their discretionary choice and undercuts their power to compel obedience, particularly when a supervisor disapproves a petition. They also claim that it prevents a swift response to violations.

Structured Responses to Violations

In several states, line officers use formal decision-making guidelines or criteria to handle violations. In general, the objectives have been to deter violations by inflicting swift and/or certain punishment or to make punishments more uniform and proportional.

Generally, revocation guidelines or criteria use the same array of intermediate sanctions available to sentencing judges as punishments for violations, including restitution, community service, day reporting, intensive supervision, and halfway houses or other community residential settings. These sanctions allow officials to scale the severity of the punishment in relation to the seriousness of the violation.

Existing Guidelines Used as Benchmarks

Delaware, Tennessee, and Utah use existing guidelines as benchmarks for selecting responses to violations. Delaware's sentencing guidelines have five punishment scales within which judges select initial sentences. For probationers who later violate conditions, the scales are used as guides to select increased sanctions. In Tennessee and Utah, supervision classification guidelines used to establish initial levels and frequency of contacts are also used to determine increased contact and supervision levels for violators.

Violation Guidelines

Oregon, Minnesota, South Carolina, New Hampshire, Michigan, Pennsylvania, and Connecticut have developed separate guidelines for sanctioning violators.

In Oregon, probation departments in counties that participate in the Community Corrections Act developed the Drug Reduction on Probation (DROP) guidelines, which provide swift and certain sanctions for probationers who fail drug tests. According to DROP guidelines, every person who fails a drug test does jail time. The first violation calls for one or two days in jail, the second calls for a week in jail, and the third calls for thirty days of local confinement. Officials maintain that the total number of days in jail needed to confine drug-using probationers has dropped in counties that use DROP guidelines. Although the first and second violations are common, the number of third violations has dropped dramatically, supporting the notion that swift and certain, but not necessarily severe, sanctions can deter violations.

Minnesota's DOC has revocation guidelines for persons on supervised release—its term for post-prison community supervision. When revocation petitions are filed, DOC hearing examiners decide when to revoke and return to prison and how long to confine, using guidelines based on the offender's original conviction offense and the seriousness of the alleged violation.

South Carolina's revocation guidelines address both probation and parole violations. The guidelines aim for sanctions to be proportional to the severity of violations and uniformly applied. Violators are classified according to the severity of the violation and their risk scores. The guidelines outline a range of sanctions (community service, residential placement, confinement, etc.) for each category, allowing probation and parole officers to recommend specific sanctions. The guidelines were not developed to reduce prison admissions; however, both the number of prison admissions and population decreased after the guidelines went into effect.

Statutory Responses

The Georgia legislature initially enacted a law that flatly prohibited imprisonment of technical violators. However, strong pressure from probation officers and judges led to the law being repealed.

Texas law requires that technical violators be given three increasingly severe intermediate punishments before allowing probation to be revoked and the violator imprisoned.

Washington's original sentencing guidelines law limited sanctions for probation violations to ninety days in jail.

Innovative Absconder Policies

Some states have implemented approaches designed to enhance location and capture of absconders.

Enhanced Probation and Parole Officer Responsibilities

Realizing that many absconders remain in their community, probation and parole officers in New Hampshire are required to document at least five contacts—last known residence, place of employment, family, friends, and employer—to try to locate the absconder.

Limited-sanction Approach

Some officials believe that drug testing has increased absconding. If an offender has failed a prior drug test and knows he or she will test positive if tested again, absconding may seem more appealing than facing revocation and possible imprisonment. But life is difficult and unpleasant for absconders. They may forego welfare benefits for fear of being located and may end up with fewer legitimate survival options. Every contact with police, however remote or casual, is threatening. Thus, many absconders are eager to end their fugitive status, particularly if their fear of long-term imprisonment is allayed.

In Washington, D.C., probation officers aggressively seek out absconders and, once they are found, convince them to return to supervision by offering to limit the most severe sanction that will be imposed. This is not considered amnesty because the violation is not forgiven, and a sanction is, in fact, applied. During its first few months of operation, the D.C. program located and returned to supervision more than 70 percent of the absconders it sought out.

Improved Information

Several states use comprehensive techniques to find absconders. Volunteers in Tennessee make telephone calls and write letters to individuals or companies who may know where an absconder is. Clerical staff in Oklahoma review records (i.e., hunting or fishing licenses and tax records) of other state agencies and public utilities in an effort to locate absconders.

Privatizing Absconder Apprehension

The Minnesota DOC contracts with a former federal probation officer to find and apprehend supervised release absconders. Hennepin County, Minnesota, Community Corrections also uses a private contractor to locate and apprehend probation absconders.

Enhanced Fugitive Units

In California, Massachusetts, Arizona, New Mexico, Nevada, Utah, Georgia, New York City, and Texas, enhanced fugitive units have been created to aggressively seek out and apprehend selected absconders. California's Parolee-at-large Recovery Units (PALRU) work closely with local police to target absconders for apprehension, develop intelligence on their whereabouts, and conduct joint operations to locate and apprehend them. PALRU members are armed, fitted with body armor during raids, and trained in tactics.

The Massachusetts State Police formed the Violent Fugitives Strike Force several years ago to locate and capture fugitives wanted for new alleged crimes, some of whom were on probation or parole. The four-person fugitive unit of the state's parole board routinely shares information with the Violent Fugitives Strike Force. The two agencies jointly conduct one or two early-morning "sweeps" a month, in which jointly targeted absconders are apprehended.

Handling Interstate Absconders

Some programs are designed to reduce the high cost of extraditing absconders captured in other states. U.S. marshals who transport federal offenders around the country fly state offenders on a space-available basis. These offenders are delivered to regional locations around the country, where they are picked up by state fugitive unit staff. The service has a limited capacity, and an airline seat must be available at the time an offender must be extradited.

Some states report that by using private extradition companies they have doubled the number of interstate absconders returned on a fixed transportation budget. Others, however, are concerned about the reliability of services and security practices of private extradition companies.

It is often difficult to get local law enforcement in another state to search for absconders once leads on their whereabouts are obtained. Several states get help from the Federal Bureau of Investigation (FBI) under the Federal Interstate Flight statute. The probation or parole agency sends a letter to the U.S. Attorney stating that it believes an absconder has crossed state lines to avoid confinement and giving an iron-clad commitment to extradite if the absconder is apprehended. Once the U.S. Attorney accepts the case, the FBI office in the area to which the absconder is believed to have fled conducts an active investigation. If it discovers that the absconder has fled to yet another state, the FBI office in that state likewise will conduct an aggressive field investigation.

Conclusion

Although community supervision moved to emphasize surveillance and control, practitioners typically continued to follow traditional responses to violations. As a result, the number of revocations is increasing dramatically and is imposing tremendous burdens and costs on institutional and community corrections, as well as the entire criminal justice system.

Violations are an expected element of community supervision, particularly as more conditions of supervision are imposed on offenders and more sophisticated techniques are used to detect violations. Violation response policies should provide swift and certain punishment that is proportional to the seriousness of violations. Officials need to make creative use of intermediate sanctions as punishments for violators. Policies for responding to violations also will need to consider capacity limits. It makes no sense to release serious offenders early just so there will be room to imprison large numbers of technical violators.

Responding to violations is not just a matter of inflicting certain, swift, and proportional punishments. Punishing violators is an integral component of effective case management. Swift and certain punishments may deter violations and hold offenders accountable for their misdeeds, thereby making them more amenable to casework intervention. The violations themselves may signal adjustment problems that can be ameliorated by effective case management. Thus, while violators deserve sanctions, violations present opportunities for positive intervention in offenders' lives. Probation and parole officials face serious challenges in the coming years in crafting rational and effective responses to probation and parole violations.

References

Bureau of Justice Statistics. 1991. *Correctional Populations in the United States, 1989.* Washington, D.C.: U.S. Department of Justice.

Parent, D., et al. In press. *Responding to Probation and Parole Violations.* Washington, D.C.: National Institute of Justice.

Chapter 2

Handling Violations of Probation and Supervised Release at the Federal Level

By L. Russell Burress

The U.S. Sentencing Commission is an independent agency in the Judicial Branch of the federal government. It consists of seven voting members, who are appointed by the president and confirmed by the Senate, and two nonvoting, *ex officio* members.

The commission's primary function is to promulgate sentencing policies and practices for the federal courts, including guidelines prescribing the appropriate form and severity of punishment for offenders convicted of committing federal crimes on or after 1 November 1987.

Sentencing guidelines established by the commission are designed to do the following:

- effectuate the purposes of sentencing enumerated in 18 U.S.C. § 3553(a)(2), which are, in brief, just punishment, deterrence, incapacitation, and rehabilitation
- ensure fairness in meeting the purposes of sentencing by avoiding unwarranted disparity among offenders with similar characteristics convicted of similar criminal conduct, while permitting sufficient judicial flexibility to account for relevant aggravating and mitigating factors
- reflect, to the extent practicable, advancement in the knowledge of human behavior as related to the criminal justice process

Organization

The commission comprises five main offices: general counsel, monitoring, policy analysis, training and technical assistance, and administration. The director of each office reports to the staff director. The staff director reports to the commissioner who has been appointed chairperson of the commission.

The staff director is responsible for planning, coordinating, directing, and allocating resources for all staff activities. In addition to carrying out the planning and management function, staff in this office manage special projects and provide public information and computer support services for the commission.

The Office of General Counsel provides support to the commission on a variety of legal issues, including formulating and applying guidelines and guideline amendments, legislative proposals, and statutory interpretations. Legal staff monitor district and circuit court application and interpretation of the guidelines and advise commissioners on statutes and legislation affecting the commission's work. The guidelines production unit drafts proposed amendments to existing guidelines and new guidelines in accordance with commission directives.

The Office of Monitoring operates a comprehensive computerized database to track application of the guidelines and to produce periodic reports about guideline implementation. The commission reviews these data and reports when it considers amending individual guidelines. The office also maintains a master file of guideline sentencing statistics that is available to the public through the Inter-University Consortium for Political and Social Research at the University of Michigan.

The Office of Policy Analysis provides research, analysis, and support on a variety of topics, including the effect of proposed guideline amendments on projections of federal prison population, sentencing practices related to organizational defendants, and substantive criminal justice issues, such as deterrence and recidivism.

The Office of Training and Technical Assistance teaches guideline application to judges, probation officers, prosecuting and defense attorneys, and other criminal justice professionals. Staff operate a hotline to respond to guideline application questions from judges and probation officers. They develop training materials, including lecture outlines and visual aids, and participate in the sentencing guideline portions of training programs sponsored by other agencies. They keep the commission informed on current guideline application practices.

The Office of Administration provides general administrative support to commissioners and staff regarding budget and finance, contracting, personnel management, library, facilities, mail, messenger services, photo copying, reception, and other office services. The office provides support to the staff director and senior managers in accomplishing project planning and budget forecasting on a short- and long-term basis.

Prison Population Growth

The commission continues to work with the Federal Bureau of Prisons (BOP) to assess the effect of guidelines on federal prison population using a prison impact model that simulates changes in average time served and size of the prison population.

In their 1987 Supplemental Report, the commission and BOP projected prison population for five, ten, and fifteen years. The report estimated that the federal prison population would grow substantially from 1987 to 2002, with much of the increase attributable to (1) changes in the number and types of offenders convicted in federal courts and (2) specific legislation mandating longer prison sentences for drug and career offenders.

The baseline projection for the 1992 federal prison population was 57,000. The estimated effect of the mandatory minimum provisions of the 1986 Anti-Drug Abuse Act increased this projection by 18 percent. The career offender statute increased the projected population by another 2 percent, while guidelines were estimated to add 6 percent. Together, these factors resulted in a projected 1992 federal prison population of 72,000. The actual population of the BOP as of 2 November 1992 was 71, 190 incarcerated in federal facilities and 8,796 in contract facilities.

In developing these projections, three variables were modeled: (1) increase in federal prosecutions, (2) changes in plea negotiation practices, and (3) departures from the guidelines. Six projections were made for each year: high and low growth rates in prosecutions, more restrictive and less restrictive plea negotiation practices, and high and low guideline departure rates. These scenarios resulted in prison population projections ranging from 67,000 to 83,000 for 1992; 78,000 to 125,000 for 1997; and 83,000 to 165,000 for 2002. These ranges set the high and low boundaries for projections of federal prison population under the most plausible alternative scenarios.

The effect of revocation of probation and supervised release on the federal prison population has not been assessed by the commission and BOP because the commission has not yet issued guidelines as opposed to the current policy statements on revocation.

Current Revocation Policies and Procedures

Authority

The Sentencing Commission is required to issue guidelines or policy statements applicable to the revocation of probation and supervised release. The commission has chosen to promulgate policy statements only. These statements provide guidance and allow any substantive or procedural issues requiring further review to be identified. The commission views these policy statements as evolutionary and reviews relevant data and materials concerning revocation determinations under these policy statements. Appellate court interpretations of the statutory provisions dealing with violations of probation and supervised releases have restricted the operation of the revocation policy statements. There is pending legislation that would allow policy statements to operate as intended. On passage and after an opportunity for judges, probation officers, practitioners, and others to evaluate and comment on the policy statement, the commission will consider issuance of revocation guidelines.

Probation

Prior to implementation of the federal sentencing guidelines, a court could stay the imposition or execution of sentence and place a defendant on probation. When a court found that a defendant violated a condition of probation, the court could continue probation, with or without extending the term or modifying the condition, or revoke probation and either impose the term of imprisonment previously stayed, or, where no term of imprisonment had originally been imposed, impose any term of imprisonment that was available at the initial sentencing.

The statutory authority to suspend the imposition or execution of a sentence to impose a term of probation was abolished when sentencing guidelines were implemented. Instead, the Sentencing Reform Act recognized probation as a sentence in itself (18 U.S.C. § 3651). For certain violations, revocation is required by statute.

Supervised Release

Sentencing reform eliminated parole for defendants whose offenses were committed on or after 1 November 1987. The Sentencing Reform Act created a new form of post-imprisonment supervision—supervised release—which accompanied implementation of the guidelines. However, a term of supervised release may be imposed by the court as a part of the sentence of imprisonment at the time of initial sentencing (18 U.S.C. § 3583). Unlike parole, a term of supervised release does not replace a portion of the sentence of imprisonment, but rather is an order of supervision in addition to any term of imprisonment imposed by the court. Accordingly, supervised release is more analogous to the additional "special parole term" previously authorized for certain drug offenses.

With the exception of intermittent confinement, which is available only for a sentence of probation, the conditions of supervised release authorized by statute are the same as those for a sentence of probation. When the court finds that the defendant violated a condition of supervised release, it may continue the defendant on supervised release, with or without extending the term or modifying the conditions, or revoke supervised release and impose a term of imprisonment. The periods of imprisonment authorized by statute for a violation of the conditions of supervised release generally are more limited, however, than those available for a violation of the conditions of probation (18 U.S.C. § 3583[e][3]).

Resolution of Major Issues

Guidelines versus Policy Statements

At the outset, the commission faced a choice between promulgating guidelines or issuing advisory policy statements for the revocation of probation and supervised release. After considerable debate and feedback from judges, probation officers, and prosecuting and defense attorneys, the commission decided initially to issue policy statements. Not only was the policy statement option expressly authorized by statute, but this approach provided greater flexibility to both the commission and the courts. Unlike the guidelines, policy statements are not subject to the 1 May statutory deadline for submission to Congress, and the commission believed that it would benefit from additional time to consider complex issues relating to revocation guidelines provided by the policy statement option.

Moreover, the commission anticipates that, because of its greater flexibility, the policy statement option will provide better opportunities for evaluation by the courts and the commission. This flexibility is important given that supervised release as a method of post-incarceration supervision and transformation of probation from a suspension of sentence to a sentence in itself represent recent changes in federal sentencing practices. After an adequate period of evaluation, the commission will determine whether to promulgate revocation guidelines.

Choice Between Theories

The commission debated two different approaches to sanctioning violations of probation and supervised release.

The first option considered a violation resulting from a defendant's failure to follow the court-imposed conditions of probation or supervised release as a "breach of trust." While the nature of the conduct leading to revocation would be considered in measuring the extent of the breach of trust, imposition of an appropriate punishment for any new criminal conduct would not be the primary goal of a revocation sentence. Instead, the sentence imposed on revocation would be intended to sanction the violator for failing to abide by the conditions of the court-ordered supervision, leaving the punishment for any new criminal conduct to the court responsible for imposing the sentence for that offense.

The second option considered by the commission sought to sanction violators for the particular conduct triggering the revocation as if that conduct were being sentenced as a new federal criminal conduct. Under this approach, offense guidelines would be applied to any criminal conduct that formed the basis of the violation, after which the criminal history would be recalculated to determine the appropriate revocation sentence. This option would also address a violation not constituting a criminal offense.

After lengthy consideration, the commission adopted an approach that is consistent with the theory of the first option: at revocation the court should sanction primarily the defendant's breach of trust, while taking into account, to a limited degree, the seriousness of the underlying violation and the criminal history of the violator.

The commission adopted this approach for a variety of reasons. First, although the commission found desirable several aspects of the second option that provided for a detailed revocation guideline system similar to that applied at the initial sentencing, extensive training proved it to be impractical. In particular, with regard to new criminal conduct that constituted a violation of state or local law, working groups expert in the functioning of federal criminal law noted that it would be difficult in many instances for the court or the parties to obtain the information necessary to properly apply the guidelines to this new conduct. The potential unavailability of information and witnesses necessary for a determination of specific offense characteristics or other guideline adjustments could create questions about the accuracy of factual findings concerning the existence of those factors.

In addition, the commission rejected the second option because it was inconsistent with its views that the court with jurisdiction over the criminal conduct leading to revocation is the more appropriate body to impose punishment for that new criminal conduct, and that, as a breach of trust inherent in the conditions of supervision, the sanction for the violation of trust should be in addition, or consecutive, to any sentence imposed for new conduct. In contrast, the second option would have the revocation court substantially duplicate the sanctioning role of the court with jurisdiction over a defendant's new criminal conduct and would provide for the punishment imposed on revocation to run concurrently with, and thus generally be subsumed in, any sentence imposed for that new criminal conduct.

Further, the sanctions available to the courts on revocation are, in many cases, more significantly restrained by statute. Specifically, the term of imprisonment that may be imposed on revocation of supervised release is generally limited by statute to not more than five years for offenders originally convicted of class A felonies (offenses carrying statutory maximum penalties of life or death), except for certain Title 21 drug offenses; not more than three years for class B felonies (offenses carrying statutory maximum penalties of twenty-five years up to life); not more than two years for class C or D felonies (offenses carrying statutory maximum penalties of five years up to twenty-five years); and not more than one year for class E felonies or class A misdemeanors (offenses carrying statutory maximum penalties greater than six months up to five years) (18 U.S.C. § 3583[e][3]). Presently the statute is not clear regarding the term of imprisonment available on revocation of probation.

Given the relatively narrow ranges of incarceration available in many cases, combined with the potential difficulty in obtaining information necessary to determine specific offense characteristics, the commission felt that it is was undesirable at this time to develop guidelines that attempt to distinguish, in detail, the wide variety of behavior that can lead to revocation. Indeed, with the relatively low ceilings set by statute, revocation policy statements that attempted to delineate with great particularity the gradations of conduct leading to revocation would frequently result in a sentence at the statutory maximum penalty.

Accordingly, the commission determined that revocation policy statements that provided for three broad grades of violations would permit proportionally longer terms for more serious violations and thereby would address adequately concerns about proportionality, without creating the problems inherent in the second option.

The Basic Approach

The revocation policy statements categorize violations of probation and supervised release in three broad classifications ranging from serious new felonious criminal conduct to less serious criminal conduct and technical violations. The grade of the violation and the violator's criminal history category calculated at the time of the initial sentencing fix the applicable sentencing range.

The commission has elected to develop a single set of policy statements for revocation of both probation and supervised release. In reviewing relevant literature, the commission determined that the purpose of supervision for probation and supervised release should focus on the integration of the offender into the community, while providing the supervision designed to limit further criminal conduct. Although there was considerable debate as to whether the sanction imposed on revocation of probation should be different from that imposed on revocation of supervised release, the commission has initially concluded that a single set of policy statements are appropriate.

Trends in Revocation Numbers and Rates

To further the evaluation of the policy statements, the commission has requested that probation officers submit the following information to the commission on all revocation proceedings:

- revocation worksheets to the court
- violation report submitted to the court
- summary of violation form
- judgment order

As of 1 August 1991, the commission's Monitoring Unit has received documentation on more than 700 cases involving violations of probation and supervised release and is in the process of developing a database to capture information regarding supervision violations. The database includes the following variables:

- original district, docket number, and sentencing date
- type and grade of violation
- new range of imprisonment and sentencing options
- Chapter Seven application
- action taken by the court

Use of Intermediate Sanctions

The violation policy statements are designed to provide flexibility regarding the court's decision whether to revoke a defendant's supervision for violations other than those constituting new criminal conduct of a serious nature. The three grades of probation or supervised release violations do not depend on the conduct that is the subject of criminal charges or of which the defendant is convicted. Rather, the grade of the violation is based on the defendant's actual conduct. Where there is more than one violation of the conditions of supervision, or where the violation includes conduct that constitutes more than one offense, the violation carrying the most serious grade is used.

Under § 7B1.3 (revocation of probation or supervised release), the court must revoke probation or supervised release on finding of a Grade A violation and sentence the defendant to a period of imprisonment without the benefit of more lenient sentencing options. A grade A violation is defined in § 7B1.3 as "conduct constituting (a) a federal, state, or local offense punishable by a term of imprisonment exceeding one year that (i) is a crime of violence, (ii) is a controlled substance offense, or (iii) involves possession of a firearm or destructive device of a type described in 26 U.S.C § 5845(a) (e.g., sawed-off shotguns, machine guns); or (b) any other federal, state, or local offense punishable by a term of imprisonment exceeding 20 years."

Controlled substance offense includes any offense under federal or state law prohibiting the manufacture, import, export, distribution, or dispensing of a controlled substance (or a counterfeit substance) or the possession of a controlled substance (or a counterfeit substance) with the intent to manufacture, import, export, distribute, or dispense. Controlled substance offense also includes aiding and abetting, conspiring, and attempting to commit such offenses, but not simple possession of a controlled substance.

The policy statements provide sentencing options for defendants found to have committed grade B or C violations. A grade B violation is defined in § 7B1.1 (classification of violations) as "conduct constituting any other federal, state, or local offense punishable by a term of imprisonment exceeding one year."

A grade C violation is defined by § 7B1.1 as "conduct constituting (a) federal, state, or local offense punishable by a term of imprisonment of one year or less; or (b) a violation of any other condition of supervision."

The policy statements direct the court to revoke probation or supervised release on finding a grade B violation. Faced with a grade C violation, the court may (1) revoke probation or supervised release or (2) extend the term of probation or supervised release and/or modify the conditions of supervision.

The policy statements outline the sentencing option available to the court on revocation based on a finding of a grade B or C violation. For a defendant whose minimum term of imprisonment determined under § 7B1.4 (term of imprisonment) is at least one month, but not more than six months, the minimum term may be satisfied by (1) a sentence of imprisonment or (2) a sentence of imprisonment that includes a term of supervised release with a condition that substitutes community confinement or home detention according to the schedule in § 5C1.1 (imposition of a term of imprisonment—schedule of substitute punishments) for any portion of the minimum term.

The schedule of substitute punishments in § 5C1.1(e) provides the following options as substitutes for one day of imprisonment:

- one day of intermittent confinement in prison or jail
- one day of community confinement
- one day of home detention

It should be noted that according to 18 U.S.C. § 3583(d), intermittent confinement is not authorized as a condition of supervised release.

For a defendant whose minimum term of imprisonment determined under § 7B1.4 (term of imprisonment) is more than six months, but not more than ten months, the minimum term may be satisfied by (1) a sentence of imprisonment or (2) a sentence of imprisonment that includes a term of supervised release with a condition that substitutes community confinement or home detention according to the schedule in § 5C1.1 (imposition of a term of imprisonment), provided that at least one-half of the minimum term is satisfied by imprisonment.

Sentencing options are available for all defendants who are found to have committed grade C violations (misdemeanor and technical violations), regardless of their prior criminal record. For defendants who are found to have committed a grade B violation (felonies other than those constituting grade A violations), the commission has preserved sentencing options only when those prior convictions place them in criminal history categories I-III. The use of substitutes for imprisonment is not recommended for most defendants with a criminal history category of IV or above (see Table 2-1, next page).

Table 2-1

Range of Imprisonment on Revocation
(in months of imprisonment)

Criminal History Category[a]

Grade of Violation	I	II	III	IV	V	VI
A[b]	24-30	27-33	30-37	37-46	46-57	57-63
A[c]	12-18	15-21	18-24	24-30	30-37	33-41
B	4-10	6-12	8-14	12-18	18-24	21-27
C	3-9	4-10	5-11	6-12	7-13	8-14

[a] *The criminal history category is the category applicable at the time the defendant originally was sentenced to a term of supervision.*

[b] *Grade A where the defendant was on probation or supervised release as a result of a Class A felony.*

[c] *Grade A not involving a Class A felony.*

Chapter 3

Intermediate Sanctions for Federal Parole Violators

By Jasper Clay and Henry Grinner

The U.S. Parole Commission has parole jurisdiction over all eligible federal offenders whose crimes were committed prior to 1 November 1987, D.C. code offenders and military offenders housed in federal facilities, and foreign treaty exchange cases.

The commission is currently phasing down its operation as a result of the Comprehensive Crime Control Act of 1984 and the abolishment of parole for offenses committed after 1 November 1987. On 17 October 1991, the commission closed the Western regional office. Regional offices continue to operate in Kansas City, Missouri, and Dallas, Texas. The Western regional office workload was divided between the Kansas City and Dallas offices. Effective 13 April 1992, the agency consolidated its Northeast and Southeast regional offices and established an Eastern regional office in Chevy Chase, Maryland, where the National Appeals Board is also located. Each of these regional offices is responsible for parole functions within its designated region and for all federal parolees and mandatory releasees within those boundaries.

Field supervision of released offenders is provided by U.S. probation officers, who are employed by the U.S. district courts. They monitor and report the activities of parolees and mandatory releasees to the commission.

Policy and procedures are determined at quarterly commission meetings and rules and regulations are published in the *Federal Register* of the United States under the code of federal regulations.

As of March 1992, there were approximately 21,000 parolees and mandatory releasees under the jurisdiction of the U.S. Parole Commission. Revocation policies and procedures are found in the *Code of Federal Rules and Procedures* at 28 CFR § 2.50. The Parole Commission issues approximately 4,000 warrants on an annual basis. Revocation hearings have increased steadily from 2,169 in 1985 to 2,820 in 1989. Of the revocation hearings conducted in 1990, 58 percent involved administrative violations of release, including drug use.

The Need for Intermediate Sanctions

By the end of 1991, there were more than one million Americans eighteen years of age or older in local, state, and federal jails and prisons. The Federal Bureau of Prisons population has more than doubled since 1980 from 23,401 to 62,844 as of 1 July 1991. At a cost of $25 million for each 500-bed federal prison, construction costs have been projected at $70 billion over the next thirty years. It will then cost between $12,000 and $24,000 to incarcerate an individual for one year (Greene 1988).

The late chairman of the U.S. Parole Commission, Benjamin F. Baer (1991), wrote:

> The prohibitive cost of building new prisons acts as a strong incentive to find more efficient ways to provide punishment and deterrence, while still protecting the public. Intermediate sanctions, also called community corrections, may be the best answer to the overcrowding of American jails and prisons.

The Parole Commission began focusing on the use of intermediate sanctions with the Community Control Project in the Southern District of Florida and Central California (Los Angeles) in 1988 (Beck & Klein-Saffran 1991). This pilot project used electronic monitoring for parolees confined in their homes in lieu of placing them in halfway houses. Based on the success of this pilot, the program was expanded to fourteen judicial districts during 1991 and serves as the model of the current community confinement program. The program has expanded to sixty-four of the ninety-four federal districts as of 1 March 1992.

Intensive Supervision Project

More direct focus was given to parolees in the Intensive Supervision Project (ISP) in Hyattsville, Maryland. The project, which was initiated in 1988, was developed to provide intensive surveillance and support services to thirty high-risk parolees under the supervision of a team of two probation officers. The project is a collaborative effort of the Parole Commission and the U.S. Probation Office for the District of Maryland. One of the intended goals of intensive supervision is to allow safe community supervision of offenders who might otherwise be incarcerated. The Hyattsville project provides a high level of interaction between the officer and releasee, averaging eighteen contacts per month determined on a case-by-base basis. Staff provide various support services, including employment assistance and social service referrals.

In February 1991, the National Center on Institutions and Alternatives completed an evaluation of the project. It concluded that offenders in the ISP group have higher revocation rates than those in the comparison group. However, this was because more technical violations were being detected. Offenders in the ISP group who became involved in new criminal conduct were involved in less severe offenses than those in the comparison group.

The evaluation team recommended continuation and replication of the project because although ISP participants have a higher rate of revocation, better public protection is provided through early intervention. The evaluation team also noted that ISP participants remained crime-free after twelve months, while those in the comparison group did not. The Hyattsville project was replicated in Baltimore, Maryland, on 1 December 1991. Preliminary perceptions indicate this program is also meeting its goal.

Community Sanctions Evaluation Project

In December 1989, the U.S. Parole Commission endorsed a project initiated in the

South Central regional office in Dallas to use intermediate sanctions with technical parole violators who have drug or alcohol aftercare conditions. The initial planning of this project established specific parameters:

1. Participants in the project were to be diverted from occupying a prison bed rather than being placed in an alternative because it was available. The intent was to avoid "net widening."
2. A warrant could be issued whenever necessary to provide public safety.
3. Research was determined to be a critical part of the project to evaluate the results of the project and to provide future direction for the project.

The goals of the Community Sanctions Evaluation Project were to (1) determine the relative cost impact of community and institutional alternatives on comparable groups of offenders, (2) identify the elements of cost of community and institutional alternatives, and (3) apply and document the use of commercially available spreadsheet technology by policy makers and administrators to identify the cost and cost benefit of various correctional options, as well as the benefit of the effect of enhanced community sanctions alternatives.

The Community Sanctions Evaluation Project is a joint effort of the U.S. Parole Commission, the U.S. Probation Division in the Northern District of Texas, the Federal Bureau of Prisons, and Sam Houston State University. The project design calls for offenders with drug or alcohol aftercare conditions who become involved in technical parole violations to be randomly returned to prison or retained in the community with one of several specific, graduated sanctions added to their conditions of release.

Control group offenders and diversion group offenders receive the same programming unless the initial intervention steps do not rectify the violations or the breach is serious enough to require a warrant.

Once a violation occurs that results in a request for a warrant, the differentiation between the groups is established. Offenders in the control group are returned to prison under normal circumstances while offenders from the diversion group are ordered to a community corrections center where they receive correctional treatment to address their specific problems. These sanctions are clearly defined and identified at each of the phases: regular parole, phase I treatment, phase II treatment, phase III treatment, inpatient drug treatment, phase IV, phase V, phase VI, and warrant.

Regular Parole

There are no contracts or outside expenditures involved in this phase. Probation and parole officers conduct urine surveillance and counseling with the exception of Alcoholics Anonymous, Narcotics Anonymous, and religious counseling, which are provided at no charge by each of these organizations. Offenders must participate for a minimum of six months.

Phase I Treatment

The parolee fails the regular parole phase when he or she tests positive for illicit drug use, uses alcohol excessively, or fails to abide by rules requiring counseling and urine submission for testing. Minimum participation in phase I treatment is six months. The parolee is required to have six urinalyses and attend four counseling sessions a month. If the parolee successfully completes phase I treatment, he or she goes on to phase II treatment. If the parolee is unsuccessful, he or she moves into phase IV treatment. Cost per day in phase I treatment is $7.96.

Phase II Treatment

The parolee is required to have four urinalyses a month and to attend three counseling sessions. The minimum period of participation in this phase is three months. If the parolee successfully completes phase II treatment, he or she is moved to phase III treatment. If the parolee is unsuccessful, he or she is moved to treatment phase IV. The cost per day for an offender in phase II treatment is $7.96.

Phase III Treatment

The parolee is required to have two urinalyses a month and to attend two counseling sessions monthly. The minimum period of participation in this phase is three months. Cost per day is $7.96.

Inpatient Drug Treatment

In an exceptional case, the probation officer may request a special condition for inpatient drug treatment as an alternative to warrant issuance. The average cost for this alternative is $40 per day or approximately $1,500 per month. Because of this significant expense, this alternative is rarely used.

There is no differentiation between the control group and the test group unless the first intervention steps do not rectify the parolees' behavior or the violation is of such magnitude that incarceration is considered. To maintain project integrity, parole officers do not know before this point to which group the parolee is assigned. Control group parolees who register violations are dealt with pursuant to existing policy and practice (i.e., a warrant will be issued). The phases of sanctions imposed on the diversion group for violations are phase IV—community corrections center, phase V—full house restriction, and phase VI—electronic monitoring.

Phase IV Community Correction Centers

Placement in community correction centers (CCC) requires sixty days of residence at the Volunteers of America Community Corrections Center in Hutchins or Arlington, Texas. The center allows furlough-type release for employment. The residents are required to contribute to the cost of the CCC residence through subsistence payments to the contractor. Volunteers of America then reduces the monthly billing to the U.S. Bureau of Prisons by the amount collected.

The CCC resident is required to attend outside drug aftercare counseling once per week. The outside counselor will conduct urine testing at each session. In addition, the substance abuse program of the CCC involves drug aftercare counseling and urine surveillance and alcohol testing.

The drug aftercare counseling and urine surveillance include the following:

1. A program planning conference conducted by CCC staff.
2. At least thirty minutes of counseling per week for inmates with drug aftercare counseling as a condition of their release.
3. Urine testing conducted on an unscheduled basis, under direct supervision.

Residents with a condition of drug aftercare or a known history of drug abuse or those who are suspected of illegal drug use shall provide urine samples at a minimum of four times per month.

Alcohol testing requires the following:

1. An appropriate level of monitoring and testing is established to ensure adequate control of alcohol abuse.
2. A log is maintained indicating residents subject to the tests, staff performing the test, test results, and whether the resident refused to cooperate.
3. A reliable testing instrument shall be used and operated by trained staff.
4. An incident report must be filed in the case of a positive result.
5. Residents will be provided counseling on an as-needed basis with the counseling tailored to the individual's needs.

The cost per day for an offender in phase IV is $31.90.

Phase V Full House Restriction

If a parolee fails in treatment phase IV by submitting a urine specimen that is positive for illicit drug use or by failing to abide by program requirements, he or she is ordered into full house restriction within the CCC for thirty days. In this phase, CCC functions as a facility for punitive incarceration. No furloughs for employment or other community activities are allowed. Failure within treatment phase V initiates immediate warrant issuance. Cost per day is $31.90.

Phase VI Electronic Monitoring

Success with treatment phase V allows the parolee to be moved into the community corrections component of the CCC, which assists the parolee in locating employment and establishing residence. All treatment programs and urine surveillance applicable to treatment phase IV apply to treatment phase VI, including phase I at Criminal Justice Treatment Consultant Associates (CJTCA) and four urinalyses per month. Once employment and residence are established, the U.S. Probation Office, in conjunction with the CCC, can request home confinement be initiated for a sixty-day period. The parolee pays a fee based on a percentage of his or her gross monthly income to the U.S. Probation Office. Success allows the parolee to revert to treatment phase II at CJTCA.

Cost per day in treatment phase VI is $6 for electronic monitoring plus $7.96 for parole supervision for a total of $13.96.

Warrant

The project goals notwithstanding, probation officers may at any stage and with either group recommend to the U.S. Parole Commission that a warrant be issued if they, in their judgment, feel a parolee's actions may endanger public safety.

As of April 1991, 310 parolees who met the requirements of the research project were placed in the pool of available participants. The pool increases each month as new parolees continue to be placed in the program.

The use of spreadsheet technology in this project is directed at identifying the assets and liabilities of applying different intermediate sanctions in controlling offenders. Research staff identify the costs associated with the six phases of graduated sanctions and use a spreadsheet to display the cost/benefit for the project. (See Figure 3-1 for a sample of such a spreadsheet.)

The initial interim report strongly indicates the diversion group to be more cost-efficient than the control group without presenting a risk to public safety. For the first eight months, the program saved 841 bed space days. This is defined as diverting parolees into community sanctions rather than returning them to prison.

Preliminary conclusions after eight months of operation indicate a high degree of success in terms of cost savings. Communication among agencies involved was enhanced, allowing for immediate responses to problems and violations.

Parole Violations Sanctions Centers

The most recent and innovative attempt to initiate and expand intermediate sanctions is a proposed federal parole violator sanctions center.

In February 1991, the U.S. Parole Commission assembled a task force to study alternatives to incarceration for technical parole violators. The Parole Commission, Federal Probation, the Federal Bureau of Prisons (BOP), the U.S. Marshals Service, the National Institute of Corrections (NIC), and the Sentencing Commission participated in this task force.

NIC provided short-term technical assistance for the task force to study the entire revocation process. The result was a recommendation presented to the Parole Commission to endorse, in theory, a federal violations sanctions center to be designed and staffed through a combined effort of the Parole Commission, Federal Probation, and BOP. The Parole Commission voted to endorse this project in May 1991.

Although the design of the parole violation sanctions center is still in the planning stages, the basic goals and concepts have been identified.

The task force hopes to have sites available in the Washington, D.C., metropolitan area, where the parole violation sanctions centers will operate in BOP-funded community corrections centers.

Offenders under supervision who become involved in technical violations or convictions of a minor nature would be eligible to participate in the program. They would be placed in the program through modification of the conditions of their release rather than a revocation proceeding.

Once a violator is diverted to the parole violation sanctions center, he or she would meet with a team of individuals representing Federal Probation, the Parole Commission, and the BOP or community corrections center. This team would develop with the violator a contract addressing the individual's needs and treatment plan.

It is hoped that the violation center will foster community support by using volunteers to provide Narcotics Anonymous or Alcoholics Anonymous counseling as well as life skills training, such as assistance in filling out job applications and learning to establish and maintain a household budget.

A research component to evaluate the programs was considered critical, and the Federal Judicial Center has been contacted to conduct the evaluation. If the centers prove to be successful in addressing risk, compliance with the conditions of

Figure 3-1
Sample of a Quarterly Spreadsheet

Row No.	GROUP/SANCTION	AUG. (31)		SEPT. (30)		OCT. (31)	
		NO. DAYS (a)	COST ($) (b)	NO. DAYS (a)	COST ($) (b)	NO. DAYS (a)	COST ($) (b)
	DIVERSION GROUP						
1	PAROLE (7.96)	2,926	23,290.96	2,971	23,649.16	3,249	25,862.04
2	CCC (31.90)	28	893.20	72	2,296.80	80	2,552.00
3	EM (6.00 + 7.96 = 13.96)	0	0.00	0	0.00	0	0.00
4	PRISON (47.18)	7	330.26	48	2,264.64	62	2,925.16
5	NUMBER OF PARTICIPANTS		101		106		112
6	GROSS TOTALS	2,961	24,514.42	3,091	28,210.60	3,391	31,339.20
7	FEES COLLECTED		0.00		607.96		229.00
8	INSTITUTIONAL COST SAVINGS	28	-427.84	72	-1,708.12	80	-1,451.40
9	CUMULATIVE INSTITUTIONAL COST SAVINGS	28	-427.84	100	-2,135.96	180	-3,587.36
10	NET COST PER DAY		8.13		8.38		8.75
11	NET COST PER MONTH		24,086.58		25,894.52		29,658.80
12	CUMULATIVE NET COST PER MONTH		24,086.58		49,981.10		79,639.90
	CONTROL GROUP						
14	PAROLE (7.96)	3,072	24,453.12	3,067	24,413.32	3,316	26,395.36
15	PRISON (47.18)	52	2,453.36	90	4,246.20	124	5,850.32
16	NUMBER OF PARTICIPANTS		102		107		114
17	NET TOTALS	3,124	27,008.48	3,157	28,766.52	3440	32,359.68
18	CUMULATIVE NET COST PER MONTH		27,008.48		55,775.00		88,134.68
19	NET COST PER DAY		8.65		9.11		9.41
	COMPARATIVE COSTS						
21	DIVERSION: GROSS SAVINGS		2,494.06		555.92		1,020.48
22	DIVERSION: NET SAVINGS		2,921.90		2,872.00		2,700.88
23	NET SAVINGS %		10.82		9.98		8.35
24	CUMULATIVE NET SAVINGS		2,921.90		5,793.90		8,494.78
25	CUMULATIVE BED SPACE DAYS SAVED		28		100		180

release, and correctional treatment, they may be replicated in community corrections centers around the country.

The D.C. sanctions center became operational on 4 April 1992, and as of 1 October 1992, there were thirty-four participants involved in the program (twenty-nine in the residential phase and five in the electronic monitoring phase). Six offenders have completed this treatment-intensive program and returned to regular supervision caseloads.

The Baltimore center became operational on 29 April 1992, and as of 1 October 1992, there were eleven participants in the program, with two having completed the program.

In the past five years, federal agencies have demonstrated their commitment to quality supervision by implementing responsible intermediate sanctions in the community, rather than limiting the response to violations to returning offenders to prison.

Based on the current expansion rate of commitments to federal prisons, there is a need for intermediate sanctions to become a permanent element in the future of agency programs.

References

Baer, B. F. 1991. When prison isn't punishment enough. *Criminal Justice* 6 (Spring).

Beck, J. L., and J. Klein-Saffran. 1991. Home confinement. *Federal Prisons Journal* 2 (Spring).

Greene, R. 1988. Who's punishing whom? *Forbes* (March).

Chapter 4

Overview of the Parole Revocation Process in New York

By The New York State Division of Parole's Office of Policy Analysis and Information

The New York State Division of Parole is charged with the supervision of a growing number of ex-offenders each year. By the end of the 1990-91 fiscal year, New York State's parolee population reached 45,033.

Parolees are released to community supervision at the discretion of the Board of Parole, a nineteen-member, quasi-judicial body appointed by the governor, with Senate consent. The board determines when inmates serving an indeterminate sentence may be released and under what conditions. Other offenders under parole supervision are released statutorily as conditional releases after having successfully completed two-thirds of their maximum sentence. The board determines whether or not to revoke the parole or conditional release of any offender under supervision. In addition, it grants and revokes certificates of relief from disabilities and certificates of good conduct and may grant absolute discharge from a sentence after three years of unrevoked parole supervision.

Differential Supervision

The New York State Division of Parole is committed to the ideal that manageable caseload size promotes effective supervision. Studies conducted by the division showed that 80 percent of the parolees who violate their parole conditions do so during the first fifteen months under supervision. The division's differential supervision initiative directs parole resources to parolees with the greatest risk potential. During the first fifteen months after release from prison, parolees are supervised under intensive supervision, which involves smaller caseloads and more stringent contact standards. Parolees then move to regular supervision, which involves larger caseloads and less frequent contacts. After a period of parole supervision some successful parolees may move to inactive status.

On average, parole officers with intensive supervision caseloads supervise thirty-eight parolees. At the end of the 1990-91 fiscal year over three-fourths of parolees assigned to caseloads in the community were on intensive supervision.

Contact standards for intensive supervision caseloads are stringent, requiring a high level of home, office, and employment visits and verifications. The parole officer must visit the parolee's home and verify employment at least once a month. Parolees meet with parole officers at the parole office at least once each week for the first two months of supervision, biweekly during months three to nine, and then once a month for the remaining six months of intensive supervision. Parole officers meet with their supervisors once a month to discuss each parolee on the intensive supervision caseload.

After fifteen months of successful parole supervision, the parolee is moved to a regular supervision caseload, which averages ninety-seven parolees. At the end of the 1990-91 fiscal year about 20 percent of parolees supervised in the community were under regular supervision. Regular supervision cases have less frequent contact requirements, reflecting the parolees' reduced threat to the community.

Home visits and employment checks must be conducted every two months during the first year of regular supervision, and then the number of visits is reduced to once every three months. Parolees must visit the parole office once every two months for the first ten months of regular supervision, after which the number of required visits is reduced to one every three months. After forty months of total parole supervision, home visits must be made every four months, and the parolee must visit the parole office once every six months.

Parolees may move to inactive status, the final stage in parolees' graduated reintegration into the community, when two-thirds of their "maximum street time" has passed successfully. Maximum street time refers to the amount of time between release to the community and the maximum expiration of a parolee's sentence. Parolees on inactive status are good risks who have made successful adjustments into the community. Parolees under inactive supervision remain subject to the legal requirements of their sentences until discharge from parole.

Although it was feasible to develop distinct intensive and regular caseloads for the differential supervision initiative in New York City and other urban areas, in many rural areas where density of supervised parolees was sparse, the travel involved in making contacts with parolees made it difficult to provide effective supervision. In rural areas parole officers supervise a mixed caseload of both intensive and regular parolees.

Throughout New York, differential supervision ensures effective supervision for parolees in all stages of the supervision process. Manageable caseloads enable parole officers to provide the level of contact necessary based on the potential for risk of violation.

Ensuring Services

While manageable caseloads promote effective supervision, ensuring availability of services designed to meet the special needs of parolees will enhance successful reintegration and reduce the likelihood of other offenses being committed and reincarceration. A majority of parolees in New York are young, male, and minority. Many parolees are challenged by a variety of problems, such as substance abuse, unemployment, and lack of education and training, that may lead to a return to prison.

Substance Abuse Treatment

Almost eight in ten parolees under supervision report past or present drug abuse, and more than half report past or present alcohol abuse. To combat substance abuse problems, the division has adopted a multifaceted relapse prevention program. The program uses a treatment approach designed to teach individuals attempting to change their addictive behavior how to anticipate and cope with the problems of relapse. Specially trained addiction counselors assess parolees' treatment needs and refer them to a variety of available resources, including outpatient services, day treatment, detoxification, and residential programs. In New York City, the division contracts with service providers to ensure availability of treatment slots for parolees; when all contracts have been finalized, over eight hundred treatment slots will be ensured.

Education and Training

For many young and undereducated parolees, employment services are a vital link to community reintegration. The division has established employment programs designed to help parolees obtain necessary skills and secure permanent employment. In New York City, the Neighborhood Work Project (NWP), operated by the VERA Institute of Justice, provides supervised short-term employment in construction, demolition, decoration, and clearing. Parolees work for four days at NWP, spending the fifth day at VERA's Vocational Development Program (VDP), which helps parolees develop job skills and find permanent employment. Parolees who cannot be immediately placed in private-sector jobs are placed in vocational training programs.

Job placement and related services are also provided by the NYS Department of Labor through its Parole Vocational Rehabilitation Services Program. Parolees with few or no job skills are assisted into the work force by the Wildcat Program in New York City, a two-phased employment program that provides individual counseling and lifeskills training in a six-month supported work program, then moves successful participants into a nonsubsidized work setting.

If a parolee's behavior deteriorates, a variety of intermediate sanctions designed to avoid a return to prison without threatening the safety of the community may be considered. Intermediate levels of structured programming and supervision are available for parolees whose behavior indicates a risk of becoming involved in the violation process, as well as parolees already involved in the process. These programs include residential transitional facilities, the jail-based High-impact Incarceration Program, electronic monitoring programs, and special drug treatment placement services.

Initiating the Violation Process

The division may initiate procedures to revoke parole and return an offender to prison for violating the conditions of parole supervision. Such violations include absconding from supervision, engaging in behavior that results in the parolee being apprehended and charged with committing a new crime, and failing to follow one or more of the standard or special release conditions. In addition, if a parolee is convicted of committing a new felony while under parole supervision, the courts may sentence the parolee to a new prison term. A parolee's delinquent behavior frequently falls into more than one of these violation categories.

When delinquent behavior is alleged, the parole officer conducts an investigation to obtain sufficient information to determine whether the release conditions were violated in an important respect and to ensure that proof of the delinquency can be established at parole violation hearings. Based on the officer's findings and a subsequent conference with a senior parole officer, a decision is made whether to (1) have the parolee remain under supervision as is, (2) submit a warrantless violation report to the Board of Parole to indicate any actions that have been taken short of initiating the violation process, or (3) issue a warrant for the retaking and temporary detention of the parolee.

Absconders are parolees who cease all required contact with their parole officers and leave their approved residence and employment program and whose whereabouts are unknown. When a parolee absconds, the parole officer conducts an investigation that includes visits to the parolee's last known residence and employment program. A violation report is prepared for the Board of Parole, and a parole warrant is issued. Information indicating that the parolee is wanted by the division is entered on two computer systems.

When a parolee is apprehended, an arrest notice must be filed by the parole officer within three days of being notified of the arrest. Within thirty days of the arrest notice, the officer must complete an investigation of the parolee's underlying behavior. Circumstances of the arrest and the parolee's behavior leading to the arrest must be fully investigated. The ALERTS computer system provides access to information about parolees' contacts with law enforcement agencies, as well as the assigned parole officer's response.

The senior parole officer is responsible for ensuring that the investigation, follow-up, and reports are completed within the thirty-day time period. If the investigation supports a violation charge, a report is prepared for the Board of Parole, and a parole warrant is issued. When the investigation confirms the parolee was arrested, but does not provide independent evidence of the violation, no warrant is issued; instead, a report explaining the circumstances of the case and specifying the steps the parole officer has taken in response to the arrest will be submitted to the Board of Parole. After reviewing this report, the board may order the issuance of a warrant. Otherwise, if not detained on another warrant, the parolee remains under parole supervision.

The conference process may also find that, although the parolee was arrested, the best interests of the individual, community, and agency would be served by not issuing a warrant at that time. Such an action requires approval of the area supervisor and the Board of Parole. In these cases, the parolee remains under supervision with pending charges, a situation that is monitored closely until the parolee is convicted, the case is dismissed, or the parolee reaches the maximum expiration of his or her sentence. Often, parolees facing relatively minor local charges will be allowed by local authorities to remain at liberty pending disposition of their case. If the parolee's case is dismissed, or if the parolee reaches his or her maximum expiration date, the Board of Parole is notified, and no further action is required.

When a parolee is charged with technical violations, excluding new arrests, and the conference process finds that the case should move forward, a report is prepared for the Board of Parole, and a parole warrant is issued.

Issuing a Parole Warrant

A parole warrant may be issued by the Board of Parole or by an officer designated by the board. The warrant is issued when there is reasonable cause to believe a parolee has lapsed into criminal ways or company or has violated one or more of the conditions of release in an important respect. A warrant must be issued when the senior parole officer determines there is sufficient evidence that a violation of the conditions of release in an important respect occurred and such violation can be supported at parole violation hearings through available evidence and/or witnesses. Except in unusual circumstances, the violation-of-parole report must be completed prior to the issuance of a warrant. Alternatives to the issuance of the warrant must be considered and rejected before the warrant is issued.

Any warrant that is not yet enforced may be voided by the designated officer who issued it. A warrant may be vacated prior to a preliminary hearing or waiver of such hearing at the direction of a board member.

Lodging a Parole Warrant

When a warrant is delivered to the person in charge of any jail, penitentiary, lock-up, or detention pen, it constitutes sufficient authority to hold parolees in temporary detention. The act of taking parolees into custody and having them detained in a local facility is referred to as "lodging a warrant."

Some parolees are already detained at the time the division lodges the warrant, usually due to a new arrest. Alleged rule violators, including absconders, are usually apprehended by the parole officer and taken to detention. When no new arrest is involved, the parolee is referred to as being detained "on parole's warrant only."

To the extent possible, parolees detained under parole warrants are held in the city or county in which they were taken into custody. Parolees detained under parole warrants do not have a right to bail, although they may be granted bail on their local charges and, as a result, be held on parole's warrant only.

Outside of New York City, parolees are lodged at county jails where they are held throughout the violation process. In New York City, parolees detained on parole's warrant only for rule violations are lodged at city lockups at the courthouse in each borough. They are then transported to a central housing unit at Riker's Island, from which they will be returned to the city courthouse for hearings.

County jails and penitentiaries, as well as city jails in cities with populations of one million or more, are currently compensated at a rate of $40 a day for housing parolees held solely on parole's warrant.

Serving Papers

Within three days of lodging a parole warrant and no less than forty-eight hours before the scheduled preliminary hearing, alleged violators must be served with a notice-of-violation form, which notifies parolees of the rules they are alleged to have violated and the manner in which they are said to have violated them and advises them of the date, place, and time the preliminary hearing will be held. It also informs alleged violators of their rights at the preliminary hearing, which include the right to appear and speak on their own behalf; produce letters, witnesses, or documentary evidence to support their case; and confront and cross-examine the division's witnesses, unless good cause is shown for them not to appear at the hearing.

The notice informs parolees that they are allowed to waive the preliminary hearing and request assistance in obtaining assigned counsel if they cannot afford to hire an attorney. Although statutes do not provide for the assignment of counsel at preliminary hearings, parolees may appear with an attorney at this hearing. At Riker's Island, the division has arranged for alleged violators to be provided with counsel from the point of the preliminary hearing.

Preliminary Hearing

The preliminary hearing is a prompt, informal, minimal inquiry into the violation charges to determine whether there is probable cause to believe that one or more of the release conditions were violated in an important respect. Once probable cause is established, the hearing is concluded. If probable cause is not found, the parolee is restored to supervision. Parolees convicted of a new crime are not entitled to a preliminary hearing. Alleged violators may choose to waive the hearing; such waiver equates to a finding of probable cause.

If a parolee chooses to have a preliminary hearing, it must be scheduled within fifteen days of the lodging of the warrant at the location where the parolee was lodged. Typically, these hearings are conducted by persons designated by the board as preliminary hearing officers. When hearing officers are not available to conduct hearings, the board designates senior parole officers to do so. Assurances are made that neither hearing officers nor designated senior parole officers have any vested interest in the case. Hearings are conducted pursuant to the rules of evidence as they apply in administrative hearings.

Board Declaration of Delinquency

On a finding of probable cause or following the waiver of the preliminary hearing, the violation-of-release report is submitted to the board within four days. A member of the Board of Parole can declare a parolee delinquent after receiving the violation-of-release report when (1) there is reasonable cause to believe the parolee has absconded from supervision, (2) probable cause has been found at a preliminary hearing, (3) an alleged violator waives a preliminary hearing, or (4) a parolee has been convicted of a new crime committed while under parole supervision.

When declaring a parolee delinquent and ordering a final hearing, the board sets a date of delinquency that corresponds to the earliest date that the parolee committed a violation. This has the effect of interrupting the parolee's service of his or her sentence as of the established date of delinquency.

Parolees convicted of committing a crime while under supervision may have their parole revoked without going through the full violation process. Parolees convicted of a misdemeanor are not provided a preliminary hearing, but do maintain their right to a final hearing. A new felony conviction followed by a new indeterminate sentence (more than one year) results in the revocation of release by operation of law, and no final hearing is required. For parolees convicted of committing a felony while under supervision, the board issues a final declaration of delinquency.

If the board determines that, despite the establishment of probable cause, the parolee should not be declared delinquent, the parole warrant is lifted, and the parolee is restored to supervision. The board may elect to hold the warrant in abeyance and restore the parolee to reside in a structured transitional facility.

Transitional facilities are residential programs that serve as alternatives to reincarceration for parole rule violators. If the parolee fails in this program, the original violation charges may be reinstituted, together with any new violations that may have occurred.

Once a parolee has been declared delinquent, the parole officer transfers the case to a parole revocation specialist, who prepares the case for the division.

Revocation specialists interview witnesses, gather evidence, and present the division's case at the final hearing.

Final Hearing

The final revocation hearing must be provided within ninety days of the determination of probable cause. Written notice of the hearing and a copy of the violation of release reports are served on the alleged violator and his or her attorney fourteen days prior to the hearing. The materials served include written notice of the date, place, and time of the hearing and notification to parolees of their rights, which include the right to be represented by counsel, appear and speak on their own behalf, confront and cross-examine witnesses, and present evidence on their own behalf. If an alleged violator cannot afford counsel, one will be appointed.

Most final hearings are held at an institution reasonably near the place of the alleged violation or arrest to ensure witnesses for both sides are accessible and counsel of the parolee's choosing is available. Local revocation hearings are provided when the parolee so requests.

Final hearings may be conducted by either a board member or a hearing officer designated by the board. Administrative law judges conduct final hearings.

Adjournments may be granted by the administrative law judges at the request of either the division or the parolee. For adjournments requested by the division, the time that elapses between the adjournment and the reconvened hearing is counted against the ninety days within which the division has to provide a final hearing. Time elapsed where an adjournment is granted at the request of a parolee or a parolee's attorney does not count against the division's ninety days.

At final hearings, the charges are read, and the parolee is asked to enter a plea of guilty, not guilty, or guilty with an explanation or to stand mute. The parolee is given an opportunity to hear the evidence and to cross-examine each witness. Witnesses may also be called on the parolee's behalf. All testimony is taken under oath and is on the record. The strict rules of evidence as in criminal trials do not apply at parole revocation hearings. Relevant hearsay and any other evidence relevant to the charges is admissible, subject to the alleged violator's right to confrontation.

After hearing all the evidence, the administrative law judge determines whether there is a preponderance of evidence to support a violation of parole. Based on a finding of insufficient proof, the administrative law judge may dismiss the violation, cancel delinquency, and restore the parolee to supervision.

When the violation charges are sustained, a final determination may be reached by an administrative law judge or by a board member, depending on the type of violation. Cases involving conditionally released violent felony offenders, homicide, sex offenders, time assessments beyond two years, and revoke and restore must be reviewed by a board member, who either affirms or modifies in writing the administrative law judge's recommendation.

In all other cases, the determination of the administrative law judge will be final.

Return to State Facility

For violators ordered returned to prison, a return warrant is issued and replaces the parole violation warrant as a detainer. A parole jail time certificate, which specifies the parolee's time credits throughout the violation process, is prepared. This material is forwarded to the state facility to which the violator is returned.

When revoked parolees have other arrest warrants and/or have been sentenced to local time, their cases must be cleared or served in the local jurisdiction before they can be returned to a state facility.

Parolees who receive new felony convictions and are sentenced to concurrent or consecutive state time are directly committed to a state facility.

Parole violators with less than one year remaining on their sentences are not eligible to earn good time credits. All others may earn good time credits, which can reduce their maximum sentence by up to one-third, the same as any inmate. All violators returned with time assessments less than their maximum sentence are eligible to appear before the Board of Parole for release consideration following the completion of the time assessment.

Alternatives to Reincarceration

Many alternatives to reincarceration not only provide options for the Board of Parole, parole officer, and parolee, but also reflect the division's efforts to work with agencies at both the state and local levels to address crowding in jails and prisons. Reincarceration should be used as a last resort only for releasees whose continued presence in the community threatens community safety.

The division's alternative programs are aimed at parolees who are at risk of violating the conditions of parole, as well as those who are already involved in the violation process. Some parolees can avoid a return to prison if provided needed services in the community, such as a more secure residential setting, enhanced supervision, or employment and substance abuse treatment services aimed at relapse prevention. The division has also implemented a cooperative diversion program in a jail setting, in cooperation with the New York City Department of Correction.

Transitional Facility Program

A stable residence can be essential to successful parole supervision. Some parolees' behavior indicates a need for a more secure environment in the community. A statewide transitional facility program has been developed to provide temporary residential programs for parole violators who require a more secure setting as an alternative to reincarceration. Alleged violators may have their warrant held in abeyance while they participate in the program. On successful completion of the program, the delinquency proceedings are cancelled. For a violator whose charges have been sustained, the board may decide to revoke parole, but restore the violator to parole supervision on the condition that he or she participate in the transitional facility program.

About one hundred transitional facility beds are available in community-based residential programs across the state, including Project Return and Providence House in New York City, the Long Island Resource Center, Horizon House in Albany, the Buffalo Halfway House, and Rochester Volunteers of America. The Providence House program targets the special needs of female parole violators and provides transitional housing services for women and their children. In addition to secure housing, transitional facilities provide a variety of services, including employment and training services and substance abuse treatment and referral.

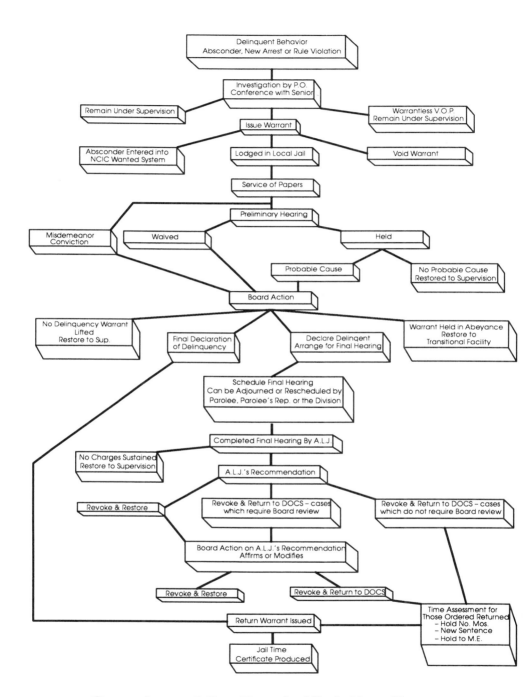

Overview of the Parole Violation Process

High-impact Incarceration Program

Through a cooperative effort between the division and the New York City Department of Correction, parolees with substance abuse problems who are being held at Riker's Island on charges of violating parole are eligible for the High-impact Incarceration Program (HIIP) operated at the jail. Alleged violators have their violation hearings adjourned while they participate in the treatment program. Those who successfully complete this rigorous program are restored to parole supervision.

Alleged violators are referred to the program after probable cause has been found (or after the preliminary hearing has been waived). Eligible violators must be held on parole's warrant only, have a current drug abuse problem, and have more than six months until the original maximum expiration of their sentence. HIIP participants are involved in a sixty-day, comprehensive, in-house drug program that stresses discipline; physical activity; military-style drills; extensive educational, rehabilitative, and vocational counseling; and work details at Riker's Island.

If the program is successfully completed, delinquency is cancelled by the Board of Parole, and the parolee is returned to supervision in the community with a condition of participation in community-based treatment. If violators are removed during the course of the sixty-day program, they are continued in the violation process.

HIIP currently has seventy-five slots. Since the first group of HIIP graduates was released in May 1991, over 250 parolees have successfully completed the program.

Community-based Treatment Alternatives

The division contracts with Treatment Alternatives to Street Crime (TASC) of the Capital District to provide an alternative to reincarceration for parole violators supervised in the Capital District area of the Central Adirondack Region.

TASC evaluates parolees with substance abuse problems who are charged with violating parole and, when appropriate, advocates that parolees be placed into a community treatment program rather than be returned to prison. When the Board of Parole agrees and restores parolees to parole supervision with the condition that they attend treatment programs, TASC monitors their progress in the programs to ensure that treatment plans are completed.

During the 1990-91 fiscal year, TASC evaluated nearly fifty parole violators; twenty-nine of these parolees were restored to supervision by the Board of Parole and placed into treatment programs in the Capital District.

In New York City, the Osborne Association has expanded its Assigned Counsel Alternative Advocacy Program to include an alternative to reincarceration unit for parole violators. The program helps attorneys develop community-based treatment plans for parole violators as an alternative to a return to prison.

Electronic Monitoring

Electronic monitoring is used in a pilot project in Buffalo as an enhancement to traditional supervision for parolees in the violation process and for those who are on the verge of delinquency. Besides enabling parolees to remain in the community to pursue employment, education, and substance abuse treatment, the electronic monitoring program helps parole officers enforce curfews and detect violations of the conditions of parole.

The Buffalo program uses VOREC VOICENET, an integrated system that includes an active radio signal component, as well as a passive voice verification procedure. Participants wear ankle bracelets that continuously emit a radio signal. If the signal is broken at an unauthorized time for the parolee to be away from home, the system triggers a voice-verification check. Additional telephone checks can be scheduled on a regular or random basis. If a parolee fails to respond to the telephone call or fails the voice verification test, the central computer registers a violation. The parole officer is then paged via a beeper and is able to immediately investigate the violation.

During the 1990-91 fiscal year, sixty-seven parolees participated in the Buffalo program. Typically, parolees spent between 60 and 120 days in the program.

Conclusion

Reincarceration is a last resort for parolees who threaten the safety of the community. In New York State, the Division of Parole works to ensure all parolees have effective services available to them, reducing the likelihood of reoffending or violating the conditions of release and reincarceration. When parolees fail to abide by release conditions, a number of intermediate sanctions and structured services are available as alternatives to a return to prison. However, when community safety is threatened and a return to prison is warranted, the division's revocation process ensures a fair, speedy, and certain response.

Chapter 5
Missouri's Response to Technical Violators

By Paul D. Herman

In Missouri during the 1980s, there was a significant increase in offender population in the Department of Corrections (DOC) as well as in the number of offenders under the supervision of the Board of Probation and Parole (see Table 5-1).

During this period, the DOC added six correctional facilities to the ten already established.

Population growth of offenders under the jurisdiction of the Board of Probation and Parole was relatively steady in the first half of the decade and escalated significantly from fiscal year 1987 through FY 1991. In addition to increasing the number of field staff for primary supervision, new supervision strategies were created to effectively manage offenders on probation and parole. Expanding supervision strategy options gave line staff and decision makers greater flexibility, allowing more effective use of community-based programs as opposed to incarceration.

Missouri's Board of Probation and Parole is a division of the DOC. Other divisions include the Division of Adult Institutions, the Division of Classification and Treatment, and the Division of Administration.

The Board of Probation and Parole has jurisdiction over all adult offenders under probation or parole supervision throughout the state. The board's jurisdiction is divided into six geographical regions with fifty field and institutional offices. The board comprises five full-time members who are appointed by the governor with the advice and consent of the Senate. The chairman of the board is the chief administrative officer of the division. The board has the overall responsibility and authority for the release of offenders incarcerated by the DOC, including their supervision in the community. In addition to supervising offenders on probation and parole, staff supervise a number of offenders participating in various community corrections programs who have not reached their individual presumptive parole dates. Thus, the basic responsibility for the supervision of the majority of all offenders in the community rests with this organization. Because of a very close and cooperative working relationship among the divisions within the DOC, strategies can be employed to effectively handle the myriad of problems associated with the offender population.

Current Revocation Practices and Policies

In 1984, the DOC implemented the community sentencing program. At that time,

Table 5-1

Offender Population Growth

Fiscal Year	Number of Offenders	
	Incarcerated	Probation & Parole
1980	5,604	17,829
1985	9,452	28,311
1991	15,252	46,123

the court had two basic choices in dealing with technical violators: continue under traditional supervision or revoke the probation and incarcerate. The courts were looking for other methods to deal with these offenders, and the community sentencing program provides the means and methods to fill the gap.

As with many other intensive supervision programs, the community sentencing program allowed for significant contact between the offender and the supervising officer to address specific problem areas. The target group included probationers with sufficient technical violations to justify revocation and those whose probation would be revoked if it were not for the community sentencing program. Pilot projects were established in three jurisdictions; this supervision strategy would be offered to all jurisdictions through gradual and controlled growth.

In March 1987, the DOC opened the Kansas City Recycling Center, a forty-one bed facility operated by a private contractor to deal with technical parole violators in line with DOC operational standards. At the time the center was opened, the Board of Probation and Parole determined who would be referred, focusing on technical violators who were being recommended for revocation. Each offender was to participate in a multidimensional treatment program that included individual counseling, group counseling, educational enrichment, substance abuse treatment, and work release. During the first forty-five days, offenders must adhere to a rigid schedule of daily activities while restricted to the facility. Visitation is limited and recreational pass time prohibited. The second half of the program includes work release, continued individual and group counseling, and placement in Alcoholic Anonymous or Narcotics Anonymous groups, if needed, to begin work on a transition back to the community. The center had a significant effect on reducing the number of parolees returned to the DOC for technical violations, particularly from the Kansas City area.

The Planning, Research, and Evaluation Unit examined the DOC's institutional commitments over a ten-year period in an attempt to identify the effect of the violator population on the system. It found that, over a period of time, parole violators being returned to the DOC had increased from 10 percent of the overall commitments to the department to 22 percent of the commitments. For a like period of time, probation violators committed to the department increased from 15 percent to 17 percent of all new commitments. Thus, almost 40 percent of the commitments to the DOC were the results of revocation of either probation or parole. Although a significant number of offenders committed to the department were committed because of new offenses as opposed to simple technical violations, the study showed that the percentage of technical violators over a period of years had continued to increase and, in fact, had reached the point where over half of the offenders had their probation or parole revoked because of technical violations, not new offenses.

The DOC began to focus not only on specific programs and supervision strategies for offenders, but more important, on policy matters concerning the violator group. There was a need for better overall direction for staff, as well as a need for greater flexibility in managing offenders. The DOC had to ensure that staff had a better understanding of the underlying philosophy of the agency in dealing with violators and that the policies and procedures implemented were consistent with that philosophy. The difference between the technical violator and the violator who had been charged with a new offense had to be clear. Policy and strategies developed would focus on the technical violator. Staff were expected to assess each offender relative to the risk they posed for reoffending, as well as the offender's individual treatment needs. This assessment process was key to the determination of what strategy or sanction should be employed as a result of the offender's violation. The bottom line was that the least restrictive strategy be employed for the violator based on his or her risks and needs.

To carry out this philosophy, a number of long-standing procedures had to be changed and new procedures developed to provide not only direction but the flexibility and ability of staff to carry out the task. In the past, staff were required to submit violation reports when they became aware of a violation of any technical condition of probation or parole, as well as law violations. There was no discretion or flexibility on the officer's part other than formal notice. No action was taken by the board or the court on many of these technical violations because they were not critical and could be handled by the officer without direction by the releasing authority. However, because of the mandate to report any and all violations, some staff would await direction from the court or the board before dealing with the matter, which caused unnecessary delay. Others would proceed to deal with the issue, taking the necessary steps to move forward in the supervision of the case. Staff were expected to handle certain technical violations as a matter of course. Procedure was amended to allow greater discretion in the reporting of most technical violations. Officers were given flexibility and responsibility to address problems and to implement the appropriate methods to resolve them as a normal part of the supervision process without having to file a formal violation report and await a response.

A long-standing practice concerning parole absconders was amended to bring it in line with agency philosophy. Previously a separate procedure was used to handle parole absconders. This practice presupposed the automatic return and revocation of anyone who had been declared an absconder. Because this is contrary to the directives that each case be assessed relative to the violator's risk for reoffending and consideration of his or her individual treatment needs, the new procedure calls for absconding to be considered in the same manner as other technical violations. As a result of this change in procedure, revocation was reduced by almost 50 percent in this category.

To ensure all cases are carefully assessed and reviewed relative to the violation and the most appropriate response, specific procedures were put in place that required screening for the least restrictive community program for intervention prior to considering revocation. Individual staff members serve as screening officers to assist staff in individual case review and identification of resource availability.

A violation decision guideline matrix was developed to assist staff in determining appropriate responses to violations and to ensure equitable decision making in response to violations. The guide outlines the various sanctions that may be imposed based on the type of case, as well as the nature of the violation. In dealing with violations, staff must carefully assess the circumstances of the violation; risk to the community; intervention, control, and treatment needs; and available supervision strategies before making a recommendation. The use of progressively restrictive supervision strategies allows for greater flexibility in dealing with the violator in the community.

Using Intermediate Sanctions

At the end of fiscal year 1986, there were 10,257 offenders incarcerated in the DOC. Four years later at the end of FY 1990, that population had increased by 47 percent to 15,108. At the same time, the population under the supervision of the Board of Probation and Parole continued to escalate—at the end of FY 1986, there were 30,894 offenders under supervision; that number increased by 52 percent to 47,526 by the end of FY 1990. This growth heightened concerns about how to effectively manage the offender population. Beginning in FY 1989 and continuing to the present, the increase in the number of offenders assigned to both the field and the DOC led the department as a whole to look at additional methods and strategies to deal with supervision of offenders in the community, particularly problematic offenders.

A task force was developed to look at possible alternatives for establishing programs similar to the Kansas City Recycling Center. Staff from various divisions within the DOC identified an existing institution in the Division of Adult Institutions that could be converted to provide such a program. All those involved agreed that the department would benefit from converting an existing institution into a treatment facility similar to the recycling center. Thus, in November 1989, the Tipton Treatment Center, a small, 250-bed facility for male offenders, was established. Parole violators and others in department honor centers and residential treatment centers who had difficulty meeting the rules and regulations of those programs were sent to Tipton.

The creation of the Tipton Treatment Center involved three separate divisions pooling staff resources to provide program development, as well as to train facility staff to help change its mission from an institution dealing with the usual inmate population to a treatment center providing intensive services to parole technical violators. Since the opening of the Tipton Treatment Center more than one thousand offenders have successfully gone through the program.

Shortly after the Tipton Treatment Center opened, a similar program for female offenders was established at the St. Louis Community Release Center. The program was modeled after Tipton's, and its development and implementation relied on the coordinated efforts and resources of various divisions in the department. The center provides a supervision and treatment strategy staff use to effectively manage the violator population. It is consistent with the overall philosophy that revocation and recommitment should be reserved only for those offenders who pose the highest risk of reoffending. The Tipton Treatment Center and St. Louis Community Release Center are alternatives to provide control and structure, as well as treatment and intervention, in an effort to address problem behavior short of reincarceration.

Because of the overall acceptance and success of the Tipton Treatment Center for parole violators, a similar program for probation violators, particularly those with substance abuse problems, was developed. Once again, staff from each division were brought together to identify a facility and the corresponding staff and resources needed to implement a structured treatment-oriented program for probationers. In April 1991, the Mineral Area Treatment Center was opened. The center is a one-hundred-bed facility available by court order to probation violators for treatment where prior treatment has failed in the community or where no resources exist in the community to provide the kind of control, structure, treatment, and intervention necessary to address the offender's behavior.

In August 1991, another such center was opened—a 130-bed facility replicating the program at Mineral Area to meet the needs of the courts. The programs at these facilities last from 90 to 120 days, allowing significant numbers of probationers to be diverted from revocation and commitment to the department.

The efforts described here focus on residential or in-patient services that deal with technical violators. At the same time, the DOC realized the need to provide additional field supervision strategies to manage the offender. In October 1988, a house arrest program was initiated; it was designed for inmates committed for class C and D felonies. The program was intended to allow the early release of eligible offenders into the community prior to their presumptive parole dates through house arrest. After reviewing the results of using house arrest, the DOC determined that the control and intervention available under house arrest would be appropriate for some technical violators—those who did not need in-patient services, yet required greater structure and treatment than traditional supervision would offer. The policy on house arrest was amended to include its application to technical probation and parole violators.

With the policy directive in place, appropriate discretion and responsibility placed in the officers' hands, and numerous strategies available, the DOC has the tools needed to manage violators in a responsible and consistent manner, while providing appropriate supervision strategies between traditional probation and parole supervision and prison. These strategies focus on intensive field supervision, including house arrest, community sentencing, and residential treatment, such as halfway houses, violator centers, and treatment centers.

Supervision Strategies

The following are a few of the intervention and problem-solving strategies used throughout the State of Missouri. Key issues are centered on strong policy initiatives that drive the development and implementation of program strategies. The combined efforts of the various divisions within the DOC have enhanced the development and implementation of supervision strategies available to staff to effectively manage probation and parole violators.

Primary Probation and Parole Supervision—Minimum, Regular, Enhanced

Primary probation and parole supervision involves direct field supervision. Supervising officers assess risk and needs of offenders in determining level of supervision (minimum, regular, enhanced). Through ongoing assessment, officers ensure that problem areas are addressed and that offenders progress through the system without undue delay or risk to the community. For probationers usual terms of supervision start at six months, not to exceed five years. Parolees and conditional releasees serve the remainder of their sentences to date of expiration or discharge by the board. This supervision strategy is recommended for offenders who can be supervised in the community without posing detriment. Treatment needs and supervision objectives of the offender can be addressed within the community.

Intensive Supervision Probation

Intensive supervision probation involves intense field supervision and case management of probationers. It involves higher levels of contacts and requirements than primary supervision. The three-phase program typically lasts between six and nine months. The goal is to avail a full range of community resources. Officer contacts (to include significant others), intensive casework, control issues, and community resources are emphasized.

Intensive Supervision Parole

Intensive supervision parole involves intensive field supervision and case management of parolees. It involves higher levels of contacts and requirements than primary supervision. The three-phase program may last between six and nine months. The goal is to avail a full range of community resources and a gradual reduction in supervision during the reintegration of offenders into the community. Officer contacts, intensive casework, control issues, and community resources are emphasized.

Electronic Monitoring Program (House Arrest)

The electronic monitoring program is home-based and ensures an appropriate level of supervision through electronic monitoring. Intervention, control, and treatment are the supervision objectives. Control is substantially enhanced as a result of curfew requirements and restricted recreation, which are monitored twenty-four hours per day. The duration of this three-phase program is 120 days. The board and court may extend program length in the case of program violations. Offenders are required to pay a portion of earnings to the inmate revolving fund to defray cost of the program.

Residential Treatment Facilities

The residential treatment program is designed to service all felony offenders with diverse treatment needs, although emphasis is placed on substance abuse, relapse prevention, and life skills management. It is a two-phase, ninety-day program that restricts offenders to the facility for the first thirty days. Concentrated therapeutic programming is required during the remaining sixty days with restricted pass privileges. Offenders are required to pay a portion of earnings to the inmate revolving fund to defray the cost of the program. Additionally, a portion of earnings is required to be put in savings.

St. Louis Community Treatment Center

The St. Louis Community Treatment Center is a residential treatment program for female inmates, parolees, conditional releasees, and violators. It provides structured therapeutic programming to offenders with diverse treatment needs. Treatment focus is on substance abuse treatment, relapse prevention, and life skills development. The ninety-day program restricts offenders to the facility for the first thirty days. Work release and community service are required during the remainder of the program. Recreation is limited to the facility; no pass privileges are allowed.

Mineral Area Treatment Center and Farmington Treatment Center

Eligible male offenders and felony probation violators meeting statutory requirements may be assigned to the Mineral Area Treatment Center and the Farmington Treatment Center for an eleven-week substance abuse treatment program. The programs are housed in correctional institutions operated by Division of Classification and Treatment. The programs focus on relapse prevention and life skills management. Offenders must successfully complete the program to be recommended for probation release.

Tipton Treatment Center

The Tipton Treatment Center offers a ninety-day residential substance abuse treatment program designed to meet a varied population of inmates and parole and conditional release violators. The program is not available to female offenders. The three-phase program is set up within a correctional institution operated by the Division of Adult Institutions. Program focus is on relapse prevention and life skills management.

Incarceration

The final point in this continuum is commitment to the DOC. However, this sanction should be used only when it is determined that there are insufficient resources or supervision strategies in the community to deal with the offender or that those strategies have failed and the risk for reoffending and the need level is too high to allow the offender to remain in the community. In these cases, the planning begins again as to when and how the individual should be released to the community. Some of the strategies outlined here may be used as part of the release plan for the offender to assist in providing the appropriate balance of structure and intervention on release.

What the Future Holds

Predicting the future in corrections is difficult because many external forces affect not only the growth in offender population but also the policy used to manage this population. To effectively deal with external and internal forces, continued planning and coordination must take place on an ongoing basis. In Missouri, the resources of not only the Board of Probation and Parole but also of other divisions within the DOC must be pooled together in a coordinated effort to handle probation and parole violators.

Missouri's current policies and strategies have had a positive effect on controlling institutional population growth and maintaining responsible community supervision. The DOC plans to continue to enhance current strategies and develop new methods of delivering an appropriate balance of control, structure, treatment, and intervention to offenders under its supervision. The mix of field supervision strategies and residential and institutional treatment programs will continue to provide the necessary vehicles to address this difficult population.

Chapter 6
The Parole Violations Process in Georgia

By John P. Prevost, Edward E. Rhine, and Ronald W. Jackson

The 1980s were marked by unprecedented, but predictable, growth in the correctional population in Georgia. The state began the decade with 12,511 prison inmates and 2,652 offenders on parole. By 1991, there were 23,407 inmates and 23,375 offenders on parole. The combined totals represent a 208 percent increase over the eleven-year period. The growth in the probation population, which is under the jurisdiction of the Department of Corrections (DOC) was no less dramatic, rising from 53,423 in 1980 to 147,952 in 1991.

The DOC budget increased from $97 million in 1980 to $507 million in 1990. The parole board began the decade with a $3.9-million budget; in 1990 it was almost $29 million. The most significant increase in staffing occurred during the second half of the decade, at a time when Georgia's economy experienced robust growth. Expansion in the prison system as well as in parole appeared to be a politically and financially painless solution to the burgeoning correctional population. No tax increase was required because economic growth provided sufficient funding. Legislators were able to satisfy voters and avoid addressing sentencing laws that exacerbated the problem.

This dramatic growth in the correctional population can be attributed to a number of factors: the number of drug arrests increased, new laws were implemented, and more punitive sentencing answered the public outcry to get tough on crime.

An apparent increase in substance abuse brought a significant number of offenders into the criminal justice system. The number of self-reported substance abusers entering the prison system increased by 193 percent from 4,379 in 1980 to 12,824 in 1990. These offenders represented 54 percent of total admissions to prison in 1981 and 63 percent in 1990. Admission to prison for drug crimes increased dramatically from 9 percent to 27 percent of new admissions during this same time period.

The new laws mandated prison sentences where probation had previously been applied. As elected officials, judges responded to the public demand to punish criminals by handing down long sentences that included many years on probation following imprisonment and discharge from parole.

Changes in the law that provided more punitive sanctions for driving under the influence (DUI) than before also added significantly to the prison population. Habitual traffic violators (usually those arrested for DUI) represented only 2 percent of those admitted to prison in 1982, but 9.3 percent of admissions in 1986. Many offenders who had received probation for previous DUI arrests were given two to five years in prison on their next conviction.

In 1984, the Georgia legislature abolished the "earned time" law, which provided an incentive for good behavior in prison. The law allowed inmates with prison records of good behavior to serve only half their prison sentences. Sentence lengths did not change significantly after the law was rescinded. The percentage of new prison admissions with sentences between one and five years did not change. Although the number of sentences between five and ten years did decrease when considered as a percentage of new admissions, sentences over ten years remained relatively constant. Unable to earn any time off a sentence, an offender who committed a crime in 1984 and received a ten-year sentence could actually serve twice as long as an offender receiving a ten-year "earned time" sentence.

The punitive approach to sentencing during the 1980s was fueled in part by an indeterminate sentencing structure that afforded judges wide discretion. The sentencing laws for felony offenses allowed judges substantial latitude to impose a term of probation or up to the maximum time in prison for a first offense. Superior Court judges could impose sentences that combine prison and probation (split sentences) as a way to regain authority over inmates granted release by the parole board. After a term of incarceration and discharge from parole these offenders were placed under the jurisdiction of the sentencing judge as probationers. Many left parole under minimum supervision to be placed under intensive probation supervision.

The Board of Pardons and Paroles and Prison Population Growth

Through a 1943 amendment to the state constitution, the parole board was empowered with sole constitutional authority over all forms of clemency, including commutation of sentences, even death sentences. The board's clemency power extends to every person sentenced under state law and can be limited only by an amendment to the state constitution.

The selection process and terms of appointment for the board's five members insulate them somewhat from shifts in the political process. Board members are appointed by the governor to staggered seven-year terms. Appointments must be confirmed by the state Senate. The constitutionally and politically neutral foundation on which the board operates has pushed it into the forefront in managing the difficult problem of prison crowding.

The Georgia parole board became involved in managing the state's prison population in an incremental and informal fashion. Over time, however, the parole board's involvement has become firmly institutionalized under an initiative now known as the Georgia Early Release Program.

The board's initial involvement in crowding issues began in 1967 (Rhine et al. 1991). Georgia's governor at the time, Lester Maddox, became distressed at the crowded conditions he observed at the Georgia Industrial Institute for young offenders. He asked the parole board informally to expedite the release of short-term inmates serving time for nonviolent offenses at that institution. Governor Maddox made a second request in 1970. These requests set the stage for the criteria that were to be adopted in the years to follow: offenders eligible for early release were to be nonviolent inmates serving sentences of two years or less.

The growing cost and intractability of the crowding problem brought every succeeding governor to the parole board for relief. The financial cost of prison crowding became clear in 1972 when inmates in the maximum security prison at Reidsville brought suit in federal court to relieve crowding and improve other living conditions. *Guthrie v. Evans* lasted until 1986. State officials estimated that for the federally mandated structural changes to the facility alone taxpayers in Georgia spent $55 million to $100 million. The prison's population dropped by almost two-thirds as a result of the lawsuit.

In 1974 Governor Jimmy Carter directed a committee of criminal justice professionals and legislators to review the prison population crisis. The parole board developed a program for special early release in which approximately 600 inmates were released. In October 1975, with the governor's support, the board issued a commutation order that reduced by one year the sentences of thousands of inmates serving time for nonviolent offenses. This action resulted in the immediate discharge of 327 inmates. It also created earlier discharge and parole eligibility dates for 5,026 others.

Another 900 inmates were released in 1978 as the crowding crisis emerged once again. From 1980 to mid-1982, 8,819 inmates were released through special paroles, reprieves, and sentence commutations. In its 1981 annual report, the parole board expressed hope that the General Assembly would adopt measures that would provide a more lasting solution.

In 1983 Governor Joe Frank Harris renewed the request for parole board assistance. This time the board chose to revise its Parole Decision Guidelines, which had been in use since 1979. The guidelines were altered to increase the number of releases, a measure that avoided for a time the need to grant additional emergency releases.

From 1983 to 1986, aided by prison expansion and a downturn in the state's crime rate, crowding was kept within manageable limits, but serious crowding in county jails in 1987 prompted sheriffs across the state to call on the board for relief. From June 1987 to October 1988, the board commuted the sentences of 6,700 inmates to time served. These offenders were selected from a pool of inmates serving two years or less and from inmates revoked for violating probation. Prison crowding did not abate.

Early in 1989 the governor announced a major new initiative called the Governor's Emergency Release Program. The program was designed to expedite nonviolent offenders through the prison system until sufficient prison space became available. The governor also requested funding to expand the prison system by more than 8,000 beds.

When this initiative began, 4,000 convicted offenders were packed in county jails awaiting transfer to state correctional institutions. By 1 December 1990, the jail backlog had been reduced to 1,193 offenders, the lowest level in more than four years. Between April 1989 and November 1990, the board paroled 8,243 inmates under this program. Each offender fit the profile used in earlier release programs—offenders serving time for nonviolent offenses and having no significant prior record of violence.

Prison beds requested by the governor in 1989 were funded by the General Assembly, but because of construction time and the economic downturn, most of those beds were not available until 1992. The board was forced to continue its aggressive release plan through 1991 and into 1992. Under the governor's program, now named the Georgia Emergency Release Program, another 3,535 inmates were paroled between July 1990 and June 1991.

Much of the state's new prison construction is targeted for boot camps. During

1990 the DOC and the parole board joined forces to direct certain inmates to ninety-day boot camp programs that had opened at two institutions. The programs are for inmates serving time for drug offenses who meet the governor's other criteria for emergency release. The parole board determines eligibility for the program. Other than outright early release, this is Georgia's first prison-based initiative that enables the board to address prison crowding.

Admissions to the prison system arrive through direct sentences from the courts and through parole and probation revocation. Realizing that its own revocation policy affected the rate of admissions, the board modified the policy to manage prison capacity; changes in revocation policy exerted a significant impact on field supervision.

Parole Revocation in the Past Decade

The Board of Pardons and Paroles is an entity separate from the state's DOC, and field services are directly under the board's jurisdiction. This arrangement enables the board to quickly to discover how its policies affect parole officers. The board's parole decisions are based in part on information obtained directly from field staff. Parole officers not only conduct investigations for the board, but they also provide supervision services when inmates are paroled. The parole board's direct link to field services allows it to receive first-hand information regarding the effectiveness of its policies and programs.

In 1980 there were twenty-four offices throughout the state that supervised all parolees. The agency employed 155 people. As the board enacted successive release initiatives in the 1980s, the legislature provided additional resources to manage the increasing parole population. By 1991 the board employed 845 people, a 445 percent increase in eleven years. A majority of these staff are responsible for providing supervision through sixty-two parole offices.

While the state experienced intermittent problems with prison crowding during the 1970s, the parole board maintained a strict revocation policy that demanded compliance with the conditions of parole. However, in the 1980s, managing growing prison crowding became more difficult, and the board was forced to examine every possibility for relief. Revocation policy did not escape this scrutiny.

Gradual changes in revocation policy made it increasingly difficult to return parole violators to prison. At the close of the decade, revocation of parole and return to prison was likely only for those parolees who had committed a new and serious felony while under supervision.

In 1980 the parole board operated with a parole certificate that cited a number of technical conditions. Parolees who violated curfew, failed to report to parole officers, or associated with people of bad reputation could have their parole revoked and be sent back to prison. Parole officers were required to report all violations. Warrants were frequently issued for minor infractions, and short periods of incarceration in local jails were imposed. The offender grapevine teemed with stories about how tough it was to be on parole, and it was understood that the parole board meant business.

When a parolee absconded from supervision, the parole board issued a temporary revocation warrant that stopped the sentence until the parolee's capture. Parole officers were expected to allocate time to look for absconders. Arrest for any offense, except minor traffic offenses, ensured parole would be revoked. A parolee referred to drug counseling who subsequently failed a drug test was also likely to have parole revoked.

As prison crowding worsened, revocation policy began to change. The parole board realized that, in addition to controlling prison population through releases, it could assert a measure of control by limiting new entries from parole revocation. One motivating factor for limiting parole revocations was that many inmates paroled through early releases seemed to be more problematic than those revoked parolees returning to prison. Evolving revocation policy sought to balance these two factors, while providing parole officers with some measure of control.

The board's role in managing the continuing burden of prison crowding eventually began to work at cross-purposes with effective parole supervision. Too often, parolees were permitted to repeatedly violate the technical conditions of parole without fear of sanction. Payment of the parole supervision fee was widely ignored. One day in jail to motivate the payment of a $10-per-month fee cost the board $15 in lodging paid to the sheriff where the parolee was incarcerated. Likewise, the board stopped issuing temporary revocation warrants, substituting instead regular warrants that allowed the parolee's sentence to expire.

The crowding problem forced the board to continue the supervision of many parolees who had committed certain criminal misdemeanors. This change in revocation policy symbolized to the parole officer that accountability for any but the most serious public safety violations was all but eliminated as a supervision tool. The reality was that the revocation and return of a parolee to prison required the board to release an inmate who was currently confined.

Between the first quarter of 1989 and the third quarter of 1990, parole revocations as a result of technical violations of parole fell from 13 percent to 2 percent of all revocations. During this same time period, however, revocations for new convictions rose from 17 percent to 42 percent of all revocations. Chart 6-1 (see next page) illustrates the percentage of parole revocations by type of violation (technical violations, new arrest, or new convictions) from 1989 to 1991.

Many parole officers, particularly those with tenure, had difficulty adjusting to the inability to obtain parole revocation for technical violations. There appeared to be a growing imbalance between coping with the reality of prison crowding and the need for parolee accountability.

The parole board realized it had reached the limits of responsible participation in managing prison crowding. Up to this point, it had been relying almost exclusively on revoking parole as the only way to sanction noncompliance with the conditions of parole. Other appropriate sanctioning options were needed to ensure public safety and restore a measure of the parole officer's authority, while relieving crowding in the prisons.

New Sanctions

In response, the board implemented of a number of informal and formal sanctions intended to precede outright revocation and reincarceration. The informal sanctions are selected and administered at the local level by parole officers in consultation with their immediate supervisors. Some of the informal sanctions are not true sanctions, but are considered necessary for bringing parolees into compliance with the conditions of parole.

The actions include letters of reprimand, increased frequency of reporting,

Chart 6-1

Parole Revocations 1989-91

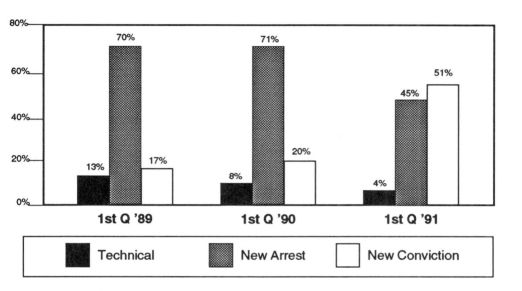

more frequent drug testing, restrictive curfews, and administrative hearings held by the chief parole officer. Administrative hearings are used as an informal mechanism to notify parolees that their violations have escalated to a level beyond the parole officer.

The formal sanctioning process usually begins after the administrative hearing. Formal sanctions are implemented when the parole officer submits to the parole board's central office staff a written review of the informal sanctions that were used in the effort to bring the parolee into compliance.

Short periods of incarceration in local jails and preliminary hearings are the formal sanctions available to parole officers. Incarcerating noncompliant parolees requires a written report from the parole officer and the issuance of a parole warrant. These steps are also required prior to preliminary and final parole revocation hearings. Unfortunately, it is not always possible to use local jails for short periods of incarceration. Convicted offenders who are awaiting transfer to the state prison system keep many jails at capacity.

Because these steps were not sufficient, more diverse intermediate sanctions were needed as part of a continuum of progressive punishments, each designed to hold parolees accountable for their behavior. Toward that end, the board has taken steps to address the concerns of the field and to strengthen the violations process.

Violations Policy: What the Future Holds

Prison and jail crowding will continue well into the 1990s. Without meaningful change in the state's sentencing structure, the board will continue to play a role in prison population management. The pressure of prison crowding will likely continue to significantly affect decisions about who is revoked and under what circumstances.

The DOC and parole statistical analysis units have developed forecasts for estimating the offender population to the year 2000. They estimate the prison population will reach 36,924 by 1995 and 49,528 by 2000. This exceeds the number of current and funded beds by 14,529 and takes into account the parole board's present paroling practices. Although the legislature provided funding for 8,000 prison beds in 1989 to be available by the end of 1992, there is mounting concern over the high cost of incarceration.

Without comprehensive sentencing reform, the parole board will have to continue to manage scarce prison beds. In preparation for this, the board is reexamining its policies. Violations policy was recently thoroughly reviewed with the technical assistance of the National Institute of Corrections. In addition, two intermediate sanctions have been introduced to provide the board and parole officers with meaningful alternatives for responding to serious parolee violations short of revocation and return to prison for lengthy reconfinement.

Electronic Monitoring

The parole board began an electronic monitoring (EM) pilot project in 1991. A review of research prior to the implementation of the project found that EM programs have operated since 1986. In 1990 there were 12,000 offenders participating in monitoring programs. In 1990 the National Institute of Justice (NIJ) reported that more than 75 percent of the offenders monitored for ninety days completed the program successfully (Renzema & Skelton 1990). Few of the EM programs identified in the NIJ report were targeted as "back end" programs—programs that monitor offenders as a final sanction before incarceration.

The parole board targeted the EM pilot project as a back-end sanction for parolees who repeatedly violated the conditions of parole. These offenders were selected because they present a growing risk to public safety and a tremendous source of frustration for parole officers. The EM project was designed to bridge the gap between the lower-level sanctions already in place and reincarceration.

The EM pilot project, funded through a Bureau of Justice Assistance block grant, began initially in eight district parole offices. Parole officers started making referrals on 1 November 1991. The selection process requires that the parolee be in serious violation of the conditions of parole. Those targeted include chronic technical violators, noncompliant substance abusers, and those who commit serious misdemeanor offenses. Their violations must be documented by the parole officer in a written report.

Referrals to the EM program are forwarded to a senior field services officer in the parole board's central office for approval. Field services officers screen requests for warrants and recommend cases for board hearings. Receiving approval at this level was critical for gaining the board's commitment to revoke the parole of any monitored parolee who violates the terms of EM conditions or other conditions.

Under normal circumstances, parole officers must hold at least one administrative hearing before requesting offender placement in the EM program. Given a ninety-day monitoring period, selected parolees must have at least three months remaining on parole. Parolees who are viewed as a clear and present danger are not considered. Those selected for EM must agree to be monitored. A final parole revocation hearing awaits those who decline to be monitored.

Other criteria must be met before a parolee can be approved for monitoring. The parolee's home must be equipped with a telephone. Those who do not have a telephone or will not have one installed are excluded. Cooperation from the head of household where the parolee will live is also required. This includes permission to place monitoring equipment in the home; remove added telephone features, such as call waiting; and limit use of the phone at certain times.

One of the important components of the EM program is how parole officers respond to violations. Monitored parolees are notified of every violation; however, parole officers are informed that minor violations during the early phase of a program are common as parolees test the system. Requests for warrants are based on four criteria: the length of curfew violations, the point in the program when they occur, the pattern of violations, and other violations not related to monitoring.

Parole officers have considerable discretion to reward parolees who demonstrate a commitment to comply with monitoring schedules and other parole conditions. Monitoring schedules can be adjusted to allow more time away from home. A parolee may also be rewarded with early graduation from the program.

Although the pilot project has operated quite smoothly, the rate of referral has been less than anticipated. The parole board has provided assurances that, if referrals are appropriate, parolees will be revoked if noncompliance continues. Parole officers are screening cautiously to ensure referrals are appropriate. After nine months, the pilot project received 145 referrals. (The pilot program was recently expanded to another eight offices, thus raising the total to sixteen participating districts.) Thirty-one parolees failed to comply with monitoring curfews and other parole conditions and had their parole revoked. Another thirty-one parolees completed the ninety-day monitoring period. It is the board's expectation that at the end of the pilot program EM will be implemented statewide.

Parole Violators' Unit

The Parole Violators' Unit (PVU) is a partnership between the parole board and the DOC. Officially launched on 15 January 1992, the PVU brings together a prison boot camp program and drug treatment. The DOC has set aside, for the parole board's use, fifty beds in one of the prisons that houses a boot camp program.

The PVU is targeted for the noncompliant, substance abusing parolee who refuses treatment, continues to use drugs, and fails to comply with other technical conditions of parole. The restrictive revocation policies imposed by the board as a tool to manage prison population and the scarcity of other sanctioning options for these offenders have disheartened parole officers and undermined the agency's statewide drug testing program. Without credible sanctions, parole officers argue, there is no reason to test.

Supported by the board, the PVU restores accountability to parole supervision. Before referring parolees to the PVU, parole officers must first demonstrate in a written report that lesser sanctions and strategies have failed to redirect the parolee toward compliance with the conditions of parole. The parole office substance abuse counselor must document that the parolee, through lack of compliance, has rejected all attempts at counseling or treatment. After the counselor has closed the file and the parolee has demonstrated, through positive drug screens over a sufficient length of time, that drug use has not stopped, the parole officer may request a warrant and referral to the PVU.

Parolees who are referred to the PVU have had their parole revoked. The program mandates a structured regimen of work and exercise during the day and classes at night during the ninety-day boot camp program. The institution's current program includes drug education, life skills, structured recreation, education, and twelve-step meetings and is supplemented with intensive weekly small-group sessions conducted by the parole board's substance abuse counsel staff. Additional programming that addresses release and supervision matters is provided by specially trained parole officers during the final four weeks of the boot camp.

A structured supervision plan that includes substance abuse counseling, twelve-step meetings, frequent drug testing, and increased field contact is the next step for the PVU graduate. An evaluation component is included in the design of the program. It is anticipated that the PVU will provide a meaningful sanction and effective form of intervention.

National Parole Technical Assistance

The parole board has embarked on one other project whose outcome will provide a framework for violations policy for years to come. In 1990 the Georgia parole board was one of five paroling authorities selected to participate in a national parole technical assistance project on revocation responses to violation behavior sponsored by the National Institute of Corrections (NIC).

Throughout the 1980s, as prison crowding kept the attention of the board, violations policy evolved in a somewhat piecemeal fashion. The conditions under which parole was revoked shifted in response to prison crowding pressures. Parole officers were frustrated when parole was reinstated. The criteria for revoking parole grew more restrictive over time. Participation in the NIC project helped the board to formally identify the circumstances that would justify a final hearing and possible reincarceration.

NIC consultants worked with the board and a representative group from field services consisting of area or regional supervisors, district parole chiefs, hearing officers, and parole officers. This Violations Process Task Group reviewed the entire range of violations and revocation policies and practices. The task group subsequently presented the board with a proposal for strengthening the violations process.

The language and recommendations in the report correspond very closely to the policy issues crystallized by the NIC technical assistance project. The task group describes the report as a series of recommendations "designed to provide a system of progressive sanctioning—consistent with available resources—that will increase parolee compliance with the conditions of supervision. They are also intended to ensure that only those are revoked who have clearly demonstrated by their behavior that they warrant such action. A system of graduated sanctions should be developed and used consistently in all areas of the state. Appropriate sanctions should be in place at each level in the violations system so that parolees who commit parole violations will be disciplined, but will be given opportunities to modify their behavior before more severe sanctions are necessary."

Acknowledging the mandate imposed on the board to manage prison beds, the task group developed a number of recommendations to bring consistency, predictability, and most important, accountability to the supervision of offenders. Through the NIC project the board was able to better understand and map which violators are revoked and under what circumstances. The board has already acted to implement some of the recommendations of the task group report.

The overriding theme behind this project—prison crowding—has brought to the forefront the need for expanding the range of sanctions available to the parole officer. Among the sanctions being investigated by the violations task group are intensive supervision, community service, and parole detention centers. Another suggestion made by this group is a rating system for technical violations to encourage standardization and consistency when responding to violations. This evolving continuum of sanctions will enable the board to deal effectively with parolees who violate the conditions of supervision.

Classification and specialized supervision also offer promising strategies for balancing the needs of both the parolee and the community. As specific programs and strategies are implemented, they will be integrated into the continuum of corrective sanctioning. For example, a parolee with a moderate drug problem may be classified and placed under regular supervision, yet moved to a special caseload for substance abusers when abstinence from drugs cannot be maintained. The parolee may then be required to submit to additional drug screens and counseling.

If the parolee fails to respond to this assistance, he or she may then be moved to an intensive caseload or placed under electronic monitoring. If the sanctions are not successful, the offender's parole status may be revoked and the offender placed in the parole violator unit. All of these transitions are specific, measured responses to the parolee's failure to comply with the conditions of parole. The movement through the sanctioning continuum is designed to provide effective intervention, yet hold the parolee accountable for continuing violations of supervision. This example represents the philosophy behind future violations policy. The continuum of sanctions enhanced by electronic monitoring and the parole violator unit offer several programmatic steps for its implementation.

The parole board, its managers, and parole field staff have come together in a unified effort to provide the most efficient management of the state's scarce correctional resources. The transition that is underway will enable the board to remain responsive to prison crowding while ensuring the Field Services Division has the tools necessary to provide effective and humane supervision of parolees.

References

Renzema, M., and D. T. Skelton. 1990. *The use of electronic monitoring by criminal justice agencies 1989*. Washington, D.C.: National Institute of Justice.
Rhine, E. E., et al. 1991. *Paroling authorities: Recent history and current practice*. Laurel, Md.: American Correctional Association.

Chapter 7

Handling Probation and Parole Violators in Mississippi

By John Grubbs

The Mississippi Department of Corrections (DOC) is responsible for all adult correctional services in the state. Its 2,881 full-time employees are responsible for the supervision of 8,870 inmates, 3,092 parolees, and 8,423 probationers.

The department's mission is to operate and manage a modern correctional system and to strive toward a self-sustaining system. Its mission is also to provide offenders with humane treatment and the encouragement, opportunity, and training necessary for reform.

The DOC is headed by the commissioner, who is appointed by and responsible to the governor. The commissioner is assisted by a deputy director in the daily operation of the office. The DOC consists of three major divisions:

1. The Administration and Finance Division is headed by a deputy commissioner who reports to the commissioner. This division is responsible for fiscal affairs, information systems, planning and programs, and training.
2. The Institutions Division is divided into three geographic regions, each housing one of three major prison facilities as well as a portion of the seventeen community work centers. The three superintendents of these facilities are responsible for the supervision of all prison activities in their geographic area. Each superintendent reports directly to the commissioner.
3. The Community Services Division is headed by a deputy commissioner who reports to the commissioner. This division is responsible for the supervision of offenders placed on probation or pretrial diversion, inmates released from incarceration by parole or other early release, and offenders housed in restitution centers. All investigations pertaining to these offenders, all programs designed for these offenders, and all surveillance of the offenders are the responsibility of the division staff. The division is divided into nine geographic areas and a central administrative office. The deputy commissioner and support staff are located in the central administrative office. Nine area supervisors are located in specific geographic areas of the state and supervise all field and program services in their area. They report to the deputy commissioner.

The Parole Board works separately but in conjunction with the DOC. The board's five full-time members are appointed by the governor. Its functions are limited to the parole and revocation of adult offenders sentenced to the DOC. It has no supervisory responsibilities for state field officers.

Correctional Trends

Correctional trends in Mississippi are alarming. Growth in both the prison and probation and parole populations is significant and consistent.

The prison population has grown an average of 322 inmates per year since the end of fiscal year 1980. Between FY 1980 and FY 1988, the DOC's prison population grew by nearly 85 percent. By the end of FY 1991, the confined population had increased by an additional 23 percent.

Although the annual growth rate has varied from year to year over the past ten years, since FY 1985 the prison population has grown at an average rate of 5.6 percent per year. The largest single-year increase was observed between FY 1988 and 1989, when the population increased by 10.4 percent.

The stacking of long-term offenders in the correctional system is having and will continue to have a major effect on prison population growth. By law, an increasing number of offenders are receiving determinant sentences, which are also referred to as mandatory and habitual sentences. Habitual offenders receive a wide range of determinant sentences. The most common mandatory sentence for an offender convicted of using a firearm in the commission of a robbery is ten years in prison before being eligible for parole. During 1990, 113 inmates were admitted with mandatory, ten-year sentences. These inmates alone will require a minimum of 1,113 beds over the next decade.

The increasing number of drug offenders sentenced to prison is another concern. As of November 1991, there were 1,613 drug offenders housed in Mississippi prisons. This accounts for 18 percent of the state's prison population. Looking back only three years to 1988, there were only 783 drug offenders, 11 percent of our total population, housed in Mississippi prisons.

A review of drug convictions for this three-year time span shows a clear pattern. Convictions for marijuana possession, manufacture, and sale have leveled off and are actually declining. However, convictions involving the possession and sale of cocaine have dramatically increased. Possession convictions have tripled and sale convictions are very close to tripling. Similar increases are occurring in convictions for possession, sale, and distribution of other controlled substances.

Like the prison population, the probation and parole population is increasing. From FY 1983 to FY 1991, the probation population grew 25 percent and the parole population grew 18 percent. The average daily population rose from 8,649 in FY 1983 to 10,638 in FY 1991.

The percentage of drug offenders on probation and parole is even greater than in the prison system. Twenty percent of all parolees and 31 percent of all probationers are drug offenders, emphasizing the need for drug testing and treatment.

In addition to adjusting to increased caseloads, the DOC must address the public's concern for safety from a higher risk offender on the street and an increased emphasis on crime victims. This has resulted in an increase in investigative work during the presentencing phase, in time devoted to victim compensation, and in surveillance time.

Revocation Practices and Policies

Probation

Although the DOC provides general policy, arrest and revocation procedures for probationers in Mississippi vary from one judicial district to the other. Circuit court judges retain jurisdiction over probation cases; they mandate the terms of that probation and the degree of court order conformity required. Standard probation conditions are mandated by law; however, individual judges may have particular concerns, such as drug use and payment of victim restitution, for which they require strict adherence. For this reason, a violation of probation in one judicial district may be handled leniently while the same violation in another judicial district may call for a revocation hearing that results in the revocation of the offender's suspended sentence.

In a typical situation, circuit court judges issue warrants on probationers based on the officer's statements regarding probation violations. The officer then arrests or causes the arrest of the probationer. A preliminary probation revocation hearing is scheduled and conducted by agency personnel. If cause for revocation is found, a revocation hearing is scheduled before the sentencing judge. If a judge is not available at the time a violation is committed, field officers have the legal authority to arrest probationers without a warrant. The officer must, however, notify the court of the arrest as soon as possible.

Parole

More conformity is found in the arrest and revocation procedures of parolees than in that of probationers. There are three preliminary parole revocation hearing officers for the state, and their procedures are mandated by the Parole Board. These hearing officers know the philosophy of the board regarding each violation type; this philosophy is quickly learned by field officers.

In a typical situation, a field officer determines that a violation has probably occurred. The officer has the legal authority to issue a warrant and arrest or cause the arrest of the parolee. A preliminary parole revocation hearing is then scheduled and held. If probable cause is determined, the parolee is returned to prison to appear before the Parole Board, which makes the final decision regarding revocation.

Revocation Patterns

A review of revocation data from 1983 to the present shows no marked difference in revocation rates. Although a slight increase in number of revocations is evident, the increase in total population would probably account for this. One significant change in revocation patterns since 1983 is the increase in the number of probation revocations for technical violations. In FY 1983, only 35 percent of probation revocations were the result of technical violations. By FY 1991, this increased to 62 percent. This is probably the result of two factors, the first being the increased number of drug offenders on probation. Recent data show that 31 percent of probationers are drug offenders. With the extensive use of drug testing equipment, drug use is being detected, and drug offenders are having their probation revoked for repeated positive urinalysis results. Another factor is crowding in the prison system, which results in a higher risk offender being placed on probation. These offenders are prone to abscond, continue drug use, and generally not cooperate with the conditions of probation. A vast majority of parole revocations are due to alleged new crimes.

Intermediate Sanctions

Supplying more prison beds to accommodate all the offenders who would traditionally receive incarceration as punishment for their crimes is becoming too expensive.

In FY 1983, the state paid approximately $18.06 per day for each of the 5,662 inmates in its prison system. In FY 1991, this cost increased to approximately $26.13 per day for each of the 8,701 inmates in the prison system. Alternatives to incarceration are no longer possibilities to review; they are financially necessary.

Drug Identification Program

In 1983, the Mississippi Legislature created a drug program within the DOC designed to provide comprehensive, intensive supervision of probationers and parolees who exhibit behavioral problems directly relating to drug and alcohol abuse. Program staff were authorized to screen offenders for drug use through urinalysis.

The program began as a pilot program in three areas of the state. Although drug identification officers are still located only in those three areas, urinalysis screening laboratories have been established in five areas of the state to make urinalysis screening available to all field officers.

The program is designed to do the following:

- identify offenders who are chemical abusers
- substantially reduce or eliminate chemical abuse by offenders assigned to the program
- provide offenders with intensive supervision
- refer offenders to professional therapy programs in the community
- provide program counseling services to offenders
- monitor suspected chemical abuse of offenders through urinalysis

Only those offenders with a documented history of alcohol or drug abuse may be admitted to the program. Once in the program, the offender is provided with special services designed to assist in reducing and eventually eliminating his or her substance abuse problem. These special services include intensive supervision, urinalysis, and assistance in finding appropriate treatment.

Offenders are assigned to special field officers who develop a reporting and urinalysis schedule for the offender. The officer meets with the offender frequently in, as well as outside, the office setting. Frequent substance abuse screening through urinalysis is an integral part of the program, and offenders are required to submit to this screening on a scheduled and unscheduled basis. A $10 fee is charged for each urinalysis that indicates drug use.

To successfully complete the program, the offender must have done the following:

- shown cessation of alcohol and drug abuse

- shown good faith in complying with standards of supervision
- maintained steady employment
- demonstrated the ability to manage his or her personal affairs
- obeyed all standards of his or her probation order or early release program

The offender who successfully completes the program is transferred to regular field supervision. The field officer continues urinalysis screening to ensure the offender remains drug-free.

To evaluate the success of the program, the urinalysis results over the past five years were reviewed and compared. The results showed a definite decrease in drug use by offenders since the program was first implemented. In FY 1987, 12.98 percent of all urinalysis drug tests for program participants were positive. In FY 1991, only 3.93 percent were positive. During this same period, positive results for offenders not assigned to the program but screened for drug use decreased from 12.14 percent to 6.13 percent.

This review indicates that urinalysis screening alone is a deterrent to drug use by offenders, but combined with an intensive supervision program, it can have a dramatic effect.

Drug Treatment Program

In FY 1991, with the financial assistance of the federal government, Mississippi further expanded its efforts to decrease drug use by offenders. A drug program designed specifically to deal with treatment services was implemented. Both drug identification officers and field officers were frustrated in their attempts to find and monitor treatment services for offenders because few inexpensive treatment facilities exist, a lot of paperwork is required to apply for financial assistance for treatment, and the volume of offenders needing services meant that providing and monitoring treatment was extremely time consuming.

To address these issues, the drug treatment program placed a program coordinator in each of nine geographic areas of the state. The coordinators' sole focus is treatment of drug-abusing and addicted probationers and parolees.

The coordinators make and build contacts with all resource agencies in their area. They explore all treatment options and services to work out a system that will ensure verification of offender treatment services. They then assess, refer, and monitor offender treatment.

Offenders are referred to the coordinators by their field officer or drug identification officer. Once referred, the offender is assessed using the Mortimer-Filkins Questionnaire and Interview, a standardized testing instrument. A treatment plan is established based on the results of the assessment and the offender's drug history. Whether the plan calls for inpatient or outpatient treatment, the coordinator helps the offender make the necessary arrangements to participate. The offender's attendance and progress are monitored through a verification system. This information is forwarded to the offender's officer. Coordinators also hold monthly educational meetings for the offenders and, in some cases, assist offenders in beginning their own Alcoholics Anonymous and Narcotic Anonymous groups.

Because the program is new, its success has not yet been determined. However, it does appear promising. Since June 1991, 505 offenders have been assessed and 433 treatment plans have been completed. Ninety-five of those 505 were placed in inpatient treatment facilities. During November 1991, 275 offenders were participating in outpatient treatment, and 404 offenders were being monitored for compliance with their treatment plans.

Other Intermediate Sanctions

Although Mississippi's two drug programs are having the most effect on probation and parole violators remaining in the community, other options are available. Circuit court judges may sentence probation violators to the Regimented Inmate Discipline Program (a ninety-day boot camp) and to restitution centers. Both are acceptable alternatives for offenders who need discipline. Both are short-term programs that temporarily remove the offender from his or her environment and are viable alternatives for the technical or misdemeanor violator.

Conclusion

The alarming growth in prison and probation and parole populations appears to be due, in part, to offenders receiving long-term determinant prison sentences and to a significant increase in the number of drug offenders in the system. In Mississippi, drug offenders account for 18 percent of the prison population, 20 percent of the parole population, and 31 percent of the probation population.

Despite this growth, revocation rates have stayed relatively steady. There have been some change, however, in revocation patterns. This is marked by a large increase in probation revocations based on technical violations as opposed to the commission of new crimes. The increase in detection of technical violations is the result of the department's extensive use of drug testing, particularly with drug offenders.

Because drug offenders appear to be a significant factor in corrections population growth, Mississippi is focusing its efforts on identifying and treating drug offenders.

Chapter 8

Probation and Parole and the Use of Intermediate Sanctions in Ontario, Canada

By Don Page

Canada is a federal state consisting of ten provinces and two territories. In land area, it is the second largest country in the world, but it has a population of less than 27 million (smaller than the population of California).

Compared with the United States, Canada's crime and incarceration rates are low and public fear of crime is less obvious and demanding, although violent crime rates are escalating, particularly in urban areas.

Statistics indicate that in 1990 Canada's crime rate increased 7 percent over 1989 and stood at 9,903 offenses per 100,000 population. Violent crime, which represents about 10 percent of all crimes, has increased steadily for the past ten years.

Canada's incarceration rate in 1990 was 140 per 100,000 population as compared with 426 per 100,000 in the United States. The incarceration rate in Canada in 1980 was 95 per 100,000.

Organization of Corrections in Canada

The Constitution of Canada provides very clear directions on the division of powers between federal and provincial governments, and this has a direct effect on corrections.

The federal government has the exclusive right to enact criminal law, resulting in one Criminal Code that is uniformly applied in all provinces and territories. Provincial and territorial governments are responsible for enforcing and administering the law, including the provision of correctional programs.

The federal government, under the Constitution, is responsible for the care, custody, parole, and supervised release of all adults (the age of majority in Canada is eighteen) sentenced to a term of imprisonment of two years or more. Therefore, the provincial governments, such as Ontario, are responsible for the following:

- persons remanded in custody for trial or sentencing
- persons sentenced to less than two years in custody (this leads to a very popular prison term of two years less one day)
- persons on probation or other court-imposed term of community supervision

- persons on supervised release or parole from provincial institutions
- young offenders (juveniles) under any form of correctional sanction

Corrections in Ontario

The Ministry of Correctional Services is the government agency responsible for delivery of the correctional programs in the Province of Ontario.

Ontario, the second largest province in land mass in Canada, stretches from Detroit to Hudson Bay and from New York to Minnesota. With a population of 9.6 million, it is Canada's most populous province and includes a vast urban area stretching along Lake Ontario and encompassing Toronto, Canada's largest city.

On any given day in Ontario, there are about 7,100 adults and 700 young offenders in custodial facilities, about 30 percent of whom are on remand. About one-third of the sentenced inmates on any day are under supervised release (called temporary absence) in the community. Temporary absence can be for employment, education, medical, or compassionate reasons.

On the same day, there will be approximately 42,000 adults on probation, 1,300 on parole, and 7,500 young offenders under some form of community supervision—a total of approximately 51,000 offenders in the community versus 7,000 in custody.

Statistics from 1980 show 39,000 community clients and 5,000 in custody. The largest increases took place in the past three years. On the surface, these statistics would indicate that in 1991 both institution and community caseloads increased at record rates, but this may be caused by changes in court procedures that require faster processing of cases.

Ontario has fifty-three jails and correctional centers, four young offender facilities, about 100 community residential homes, and 129 probation offices. Extensive use is made of community agencies and volunteers.

Probation in Ontario

Canadian law allows judges to impose suspended sentences with probation for almost any offense. The law requires the court to suspend the passing of a sentence and place the offender on probation subject to certain conditions imposed by the court. Only the judge can specify conditions, and an actual sentence is not imposed. Probation orders may be up to three years. Probation may also be combined with a prison sentence or a fine; it may also be part of a discharge process where the accused is found guilty, but a conviction is not registered.

On breach of probation, the accused must be brought back before court on a charge of willful failure to comply with a probation order. The charge must be proven, including proof of "willfulness," which can be difficult to prove. Once the charge is proven, the probationer is sentenced for the offense of breach of probation, which holds a maximum penalty of six months in jail and/or a $2,000 fine. The revocation process begins after sentencing.

To commence revocation, the probation officer must report the matter to the crown attorney (a position similar to district attorney in the United States). If the crown attorney so directs, a revocation application is filed with the original sentencing judge, who may or may not agree to proceed. If the revocation goes forward and the violation is proven, the judge will cancel the probation order and impose a sentence for the original offense.

This complex procedure virtually ensures that revocation is rarely used. A majority of probation breaches in Ontario are dealt with via the charge of willful failure to comply. The result is usually a short jail term or continued probation, with or without added conditions.

Correctional Services policy in regard to enforcement of probation orders states the following:

1. The probation and parole officer (PPO) shall ensure that probationers comply with orders made by the court, and when they do not, shall take action by way of increased supervision, variation, or enforcement as may be appropriate.
2. In cases of minor violations, it is not always necessary to advise the court.
3. Provided the safety of the public is not jeopardized and the possibility of successful adjustment exists, the PPO may attempt to remedy the situation by issuing a verbal and/or written warning, increasing supervision, or attempting other interventions.
4. In some cases where the condition is vague or impossible to enforce, the PPO will proceed by way of variation rather than with a willful failure to comply charge. When a PPO believes a probationer has willfully failed or refused to comply with a condition of the order, a charge of breach of probation should be laid.
5. It is not enough for the PPO to decide that the probationer deserves to be charged. It must be established that the violation is both willful and provable in court, otherwise there is no point in proceeding with the charge.

Since charges of willful failure may also be laid by police officers without the knowledge of the probation officer, it is difficult to obtain useful statistics on probation breaches. It is generally accepted that willful failure charges are laid on approximately 15 percent of the probation caseload.

The 15 percent rate has been relatively stable for many years despite a continuing increase in the use of probation by the courts. Trends in institutional population size (both increases and decreases) have had no discernable affect on revocation or breach activity.

Parole in Ontario

The Ontario Board of Parole is responsible for granting, suspending, and revoking parole of adults incarcerated in Ontario correctional facilities.

Inmates are automatically eligible for parole after completing one-third of their sentence and may apply for parole "by exception" at any time—even on the day they are admitted. Because sentences in Ontario prisons are short—they cannot exceed two years less one day—and many offenders apply for parole by exception, the Board of Parole must review and act very quickly.

The Ontario Board of Parole is a regionalized organization with five offices serving localized geographic areas. It has eighteen full-time members and about 100 local community members. Supervision of parolees is carried out by PPOs.

In the case of noncompliance with parole conditions, policy requires the board "to assess if there are reasonable/probable grounds to believe parolee has failed to observe parole terms and if there has been significant deterioration in circumstances/conduct of parolee."

The PPO supervising the case is required to report noncompliance to the board or the board itself may receive information that indicates noncompliance. Noncompliance could include the following:

- trends in PPO reports that indicate gradual deterioration in parole situation
- PPO report of sudden serious breakdown in behavior
- report received through PPO from police following arrest, conviction, or placement in custody
- contacts with significant others (family, victim, friends, employment services, etc.) of a negative development in parole situation
- negative information received from any other source
- significant changes in parole circumstances, such as when the parolee requests return to custody, the parolee is no longer eligible to be on parole, a technical error in the parolee's sentence calculation, or a breakdown in the parolee's release plan

On receiving a report of noncompliance, the board may suspend parole and authorize the issuance of a warrant of apprehension under the following circumstances:

- there are reasonable or probable grounds to believe the parolee has failed to observe parole terms or conditions
- the continued release of the offender on parole would constitute undue risk or danger to society
- reincarceration will prevent noncompliance with parole conditions or deterioration in behavior
- continued release on parole is no longer possible because of circumstances beyond the parolee's control

Following suspension of parole and return to custody, the board will review the reasons for suspension, determine if a violation occurred and the nature of the violation, and render a decision to revoke parole, continue parole and release from custody, or defer a decision pending receipt of more information. The parolee normally will appear at the hearing where these decisions are made.

If parole is continued, the board may add more restrictive conditions, such as increased reporting. For the purpose of classification, all parolees in Ontario are considered maximum supervision cases.

On any given day there are about 1,300 adults on parole in Ontario, and the board processes about 10,000 cases per year. The success rate ranges from 82 to 85 percent and has remained consistent for the past ten years. Some 5 to 8 percent of the revoked cases are revoked as a result of the parolee committing further offenses. As in probation, population pressures in institutions have no affect on parole granting or revocation because the board is an independent body.

Use of Intermediate Sanctions

The term "intermediate sanctions" has not yet entered the correctional vocabulary in Ontario, and such sanctions are not used when dealing with probation or parole revocations. However, many intermediate-sanction-type programs exist in Ontario and have for many years.

Intensive Supervision

Ontario uses a risk/need instrument to assess each probation case and assign a supervision level. All parole cases and those probation cases ranking high on the scale are termed "maximum cases" and by policy must receive close supervision, such as frequent reporting, contact with the PPO through family home visits, etc. However, there is no special unit, no reduced caseloads, and no twenty-four-hour monitoring of cases, as in most U.S. intensive supervision programs.

Weekend Sentences

Judges may order up to ninety days to be served on weekends with probation in effect at all other times. This is one area where crowding in jails has led to the use of weekend work or treatment programs as an alternative to actually serving time. The jail superintendent may grant the weekend inmate a temporary absence pass to work on a supervised project or attend a treatment program. The probation officer is not involved in this process.

Restitution and Community Service

More than 25 percent of probation orders contain an order for community service, and another 25 percent have restitution orders attached to them. These are major programs in Ontario. The Ministry of Correctional Services contracts with a wide variety of community agencies to coordinate the delivery of these services. Failure to perform community service or pay restitution are among the most common probation breaches.

Community Residential Programs

Close supervision in a community residence is not a judicial option for adult offenders, but such placements are used extensively by institutions for housing offenders on temporary absence (supervised release). Many residences offer intensive counseling and treatment programs.

Electronic Monitoring

A small project during 1989-90 tested the use of electronic monitoring (EM) but has been discontinued. The project, which involved offenders under supervised release, was not and is not an option available to the courts. The program was discontinued because it appeared to "widen the net," and there was little public pressure or political will for such programs. Generally, EM programs are too intrusive for Canadian tastes.

Urinalysis and Drug Testing

Offenders on probation, parole, or supervised release are not required to submit to any form of drug screening because this practice is seen as intrusive and not presently within the scope of law. In some community residences and institutions, when there is reason to believe drugs have been used, an offender may be asked to submit a urine sample, but if he or she declines, no action is taken.

Boot Camps

The concept of boot camps is foreign to Canada, even in its military forces. Although Ontario and many other provinces operate bush camps and wilderness camps for sentenced offenders, these camps operate in a treatment/rehabilitative mode and provide leadership training. They are generally reserved for less recalcitrant and disruptive inmates.

Attendance Centers

Ontario has plans to experiment with a day reporting center, an attendance-type program for unemployed inmates released on temporary absence. Daily reports and involvement in educational and counseling programs would make this an intensive supervision program. Participation in the program could also be used as a sanction for probationers or parolees who have violated conditions of their release. Placement in the program would be through a referral from the PPO or the institution, rather than through court order.

Summary

The nature of criminal and correctional law in Canada combined with political philosophies and public attitudes has not required much development of intermediate sanctions. Some such sanctions, although not recognized under the term "intermediate sanctions," do exist and are used; others may never be implemented in Canada.

Revocation activity in probation and parole has been consistent for the past decade. Change of procedures or the introduction of new sanctions have not been necessary. For the most part, both probation and parole operate independent of institutional population pressures. The one instance where intermediate-sanction-type programs are used as a direct result of institutional pressures has been the release of sentenced inmates under temporary absence conditions.

It remains to be seen if steady increase in crime rates, particularly of violent crimes, will cause politicians, courts, and the public in Ontario to view the use of intrusive programs and intensive surveillance as preferred alternatives to the present rehabilitative and treatment-oriented approach.

Addendum

Since this article was prepared, the Federal Department of Justice in Canada has released a consultation paper on intermediate sanctions (9 December 1991). The paper recommends an expanded menu of intermediate sanctions that would put into effect a legislated statement of purpose and principles in sentencing. The paper emphasizes that incarceration should be used with restraint and that escalating levels of community sanction and control should be available and incorporated into sentencing patterns.

The proposals are now going through an extensive consultation process. Although community correctional agencies and provincial jurisdictions responsible for corrections are supporting the intent of the proposals, they acknowledge that a lack of funding from the federal government for expanded community alternatives make implementation dubious.

Chapter 9

Managing Probation and Parole Violators in South Carolina

By Richard Stroker

South Carolina's Department of Probation, Parole, and Pardon Services (SCDPPPS) supervises 41,000 offenders. Approximately 84 percent of the offenders are on probation, 13 percent are on parole, and 3 percent are on various early release programs.

Offenders, who are located throughout the state's forty-six counties, are supervised from individual offices located within each county. These county offices report to one of six regional offices, which, in turn, reports to the central office in Columbia. Each of the six regions is made up of four to nine counties and is further structured so that none of the state's sixteen judicial circuits crosses regional lines.

This arrangement promotes positive relationships with the General Session's judicial personnel by keeping to a minimum the number of staff from SCDPPPS with which each judge needs to interact. This leads to agreement over, and familiarity with, procedures involving the judiciary and SCDPPPS personnel. It also results in consistent delivery of information. General Session judges are the final revoking authority for probation cases, so it is important in the department's efforts to revise its administrative hearings process and make greater use of intermediate sanctions that the judiciary be confident in the department's professionalism and ability to make appropriate recommendations to the court.

The SCDPPPS is divided functionally into four divisions: executive, administrative, paroles and pardons, and operations. The Board of Probation, Parole, and Pardon Services is a separate entity. It has sole authority to grant paroles and pardons within the state and provides administrative oversight and policy direction to the department.

Developing a Philosophy and Guidelines

The SCDPPPS was one of several jurisdictions to receive technical assistance from the Center for Effective Public Policy and COSMOS, under a grant from the National Institute of Corrections, to study its handling of parole violators. An overall philosophy regarding the handling of violations that could be clearly communicated to all staff needed to be developed. As it stood, there was little specific direction as to precisely which response would be the most appropriate for any particular violation, and it was generally left up to the agent and his or her supervisor to fashion a remedy or response.

Guidelines for handling parole violators were developed to make responses to similar violations across the state consistent, advance the idea of proportionality in responding to violations, and account for both the severity of the violation and the risk posed by the offender to the community when considering a response.

The Continuum of Sanctions

The SCDPPPS has developed an array of tools to be used in response to various types of violations. A particular offender is matched with a response that is reasoned, necessary, and appropriate. Agents recommend revocation only when all appropriate options have been exhausted or when there have been severe violations of the conditions of supervision.

Offenders who have violated a condition of supervision are formally and immediately notified by their supervising agent following the discovery of the violation. The agent's responses should be commensurate with the nature of the violation. Any consideration of a change in the conditions of supervision is formally presented by the agent to the agent's immediate supervisor and then documented. Agents are expected to maintain offenders under the least restrictive supervision conditions required to address the individual offender's circumstances.

Being allowed to remain in the community under supervision enables the offender to maintain family and social ties, continue to work or seek gainful employment, pay restitution to victims, aid his or her community through public service work, and have access to various social service providers.

Besides the rehabilitative advantages inherent in keeping the offender in the community, there are also economic advantages. The average cost of keeping an inmate in prison in South Carolina during fiscal year 1990 was $12,707; during that same period of time maintaining an offender on standard community supervision cost only $658. In FY 1990 there were 10,471 admissions to the South Carolina Department of Corrections (DOC). Of this number, 2,204 were admitted because of probation revocations (1,829 for technical violations and 375 for new offenses) and 436 were admitted for parole revocations (330 for technical violations and 106 for new offenses).

The total cost to the state for maintaining these offenders in prison for one year was $33,546,480. The cost to the state for maintaining these same offenders on community supervision would have been $1,737,120. Thus, the state spent $31,809,360 more to incarcerate offenders than it would to keep offenders under community supervision. If those offenders who were returned to prison as a result of technical violations were retained in community supervision, the state would have saved $26,013,791. These figures do not include the additional benefit of having some offenders pay city, county, state, and federal taxes and help support their families.

The State of South Carolina passed the Omnibus Criminal Justice Improvements Act on 3 June 1986. The act is a response to prison crowding and recognizes that community supervision is a sound investment from both public safety and economic standpoints. It spurred the creation of a series of programs representing intermediate sanctions falling between traditional probation and incarceration.

Because many admissions to the South Carolina DOC are offenders who were formally under the supervision of the SCDPPPS and who have had their probation or parole revoked, programs were developed to minimize the number of offenders returned from the SCDPPPS to the DOC. The programs are targeted at offenders whose behavior indicates they would benefit from additional structure during their supervision period.

The Administrative Hearing Process

The department's administrative hearing process, wherein alleged offender violations of the conditions of supervision are heard by neutral hearing officers, will have its greatest effect in the area of proceedings for revocations for technical violations. By providing agents and hearing officers, as well as the board and judiciary, with a variety of possible responses along a continuum of sanctions, many offenders at risk of revocation may be maintained in their community.

The purpose of community supervision is to selectively intervene with offenders so as to reduce the likelihood of serious future criminal activity. In carrying out this responsibility, the SCDPPPS is mindful of both the risks an offender may pose to the community, as well as the individual problems an offender may have.

The administrative hearing process is intended to assist the department in accomplishing its broader purposes, and it reflects the department's belief that community supervision is the most appropriate criminal justice sanction for the vast majority of adult criminal offenders. Thus, the SCDPPPS strives to maintain offenders in their communities, even when they violate probation or parole conditions. This effort includes appropriate guidance from the supervising agent, referral and follow-up to community resources when specialized problems are apparent, and presentation of the offender before a SCDPPPS hearing officer with a recommendation for one of the available options in the continuum of sanctions.

Generally, offenders may be categorized into three groups. The first, and probably largest, group presents no particular problems during supervision. Offenders in this group report as scheduled; maintain a stable residence and employment; abide by the conditions of their supervision program; pay their fees, fines, and/or restitution; and generally comply with their agent's instructions.

The second and smallest group comprises offenders who are not likely to succeed under supervision regardless of the steps taken by the agent to maintain them in the community. Although many offenders can succeed under supervision if enough time, effort, and resources are devoted to them, for some offenders, incarceration in prison is the only reasonable option given concern for the safety of the community.

The third group is the intended primary target of the administrative hearings process. Offenders in this group generally do not pose a risk to public safety but have begun to demonstrate a pattern of disregard for the conditions of supervision or the instructions of the agents. The agents are instructed to interrupt this pattern through early intervention via the administrative hearing process.

The violation process provides the line agent with an objective, fair, and speedy route for dealing with troublesome offenders. Agents are given clear goals and expectations for the process. Goals include the following:

- promote appropriate and proportional responses, as well as internal consistency, in the handling of violations by setting forth broad departmental expectations
- establish a framework and guidelines within which agents, hearing officers, the board, and courts can exercise their discretion in a meaningful way
- generate workable and innovative methods of responding to violations that benefit the offender without presenting undue risk to the community

The expectation is that stressing early intervention and appropriately measured responses will reduce the number of offenders being returned to prison. Only when all available and reasonable options have been exhausted, absent severe violation of the conditions of supervision, will an agent make a recommendation for revocation.

Violations of any nature are "staffed" by the supervising agent and his or her immediate supervisor. Staffing is an assessment by the agent and supervisor of the case. All staffed violations are categorized according to violation level and risk level. The SCDPPPS has developed a sanction/recommendation outline designed to help agents recognize the appropriateness of various options available for dealing with violations. The outline incorporates the agency's expectations as to the nature of agent-supervisor staffing that deal with violations. These expectations are as follows:

1. The agent must attempt to actively respond to the offender's behavior.
2. The response to a violation must focus on the severity of the violation and the risk posed by the offender to the community.
3. All available community responses or sanctions should be considered to keep the offender in the community.
4. The least onerous response that satisfies the situation should be employed.
5. There should be a consistency of response such that similar situations result in similar dispositions.
6. Any consideration of a change in the conditions of supervision is to be formally staffed and documented with the agent's supervisor.

Recording, Tracking, and Analyzing Violations

The staffing/violation report form and associated computer programs capture, as simply as possible, the outcome of each and every violation that presents itself. Capturing and analyzing staffing interactions, recommendations, and dispositions for each violation is likely to lead to efficient and effective responses at the earliest possible time in the violations process.

A system of violation categorization is used to collect data that are consistent in meaning across the state. Violations are coded to reflect the seriousness of the violation and the degree of risk posed to the community by the offender. Serious (category A) violations include new convictions in General Sessions court; the third, or greater, occurrence of technical violations that demonstrate an inability to conform to the requirements of community supervision; the second, or subsequent, conviction in Magistrate's court (up to thirty days confinement or a $200 fine) for the same or similar offense; or a number of special technical violations, such as a violation involving a weapon or violence or failure to submit to a blood test or urinalysis. Revocation for a category A violation is considered reasonable.

Category B violations, such as Magistrate's Court convictions or failure to report for two consecutive reporting periods, are considered less serious than category A violations and permit the agent to pursue intermediate sanctions or programs for the offender that cannot generally be accomplished by the agent at his or her level.

Category C violations constitute minor violations, and the agent is expected to resolve these issues.

The violations guidelines reflect the risk the individual offender is believed to pose to the community. This risk level is also reflected in three categories: A, B, and C. As with violation severity responses, differential responses are based on risk, so that as risk increases, so does supervision or programmatic responses. Combining information about the severity of the violation and the individual risk believed to be present allows for reasoned and informed violation decisions at each level of the violation process, and it allows all personnel to operate within established boundaries, thus promoting consistency.

If the staffing interaction results in a recommendation requiring approval beyond the supervisor's level, the offender is scheduled for an administrative hearing by the agent.

Warrants and Citations

Agents have the authority and duty to issue either a warrant or a citation to establish legal jurisdiction and to help ensure an offender's appearance at the hearing. A warrant requires that the offender be arrested and placed in a local detention facility until the violation matter is resolved.

A citation is a written order, made on behalf of the state, commanding a person to appear at a specific time, date, and place. Citations are part of the legal process that establishes jurisdiction for the court. They are issued when it appears that the offender does not present an undue risk to the community and is unlikely to leave or flee from his or her present residence or jurisdiction. Since it is not uncommon for local jails to be operating under crowded conditions, agents are encouraged to use citations, which do not require imprisonment while waiting for a hearing, to establish jurisdiction whenever it is reasonably prudent to do so.

The Hearing

The administrative hearing itself follows a minimum forty-eight-hour written notification to the offender of the violation. Offenders may waive this notification if they so desire. They have the opportunity to be heard in person, present witnesses and documentary evidence, have legal counsel present at their own expense, confront and cross-examine adverse witnesses within the bounds of reasonableness and safety, and receive written statements by a neutral and detached fact finder as to the evidence relied on in making the decision. All hearings are tape recorded and preserved for three years. Any decision by the hearing officer that could result in incarceration, or that is beyond the statutory authority of the department, must be forwarded to either a judge or the board for a final hearing.

SCDPPPS agents are trained in the department's expectations and receive ongoing training on new developments as the program expands. When the program was first established, hearing officers heard only violations involving parolees because they were fewer in number, and the SCDPPPS had final revocation authority over their cases. As the program has grown, the number of hearing officers has increased from three to eight, and they now hear all violation cases involving parolees, and early releasees and probation violations in the major urban areas of the state (Columbia, Charleston, Greenville-Spartanburg), as well as in certain other judicial districts, as judges have learned of the program and invited the department's participation.

Administrative hearings are held to determine if probable cause exists that a violation of the conditions of supervision has been committed, based on the preponderance of evidence. If it is found that probable cause does exist, the hearing officer can either dispose of the situation with a variety of responses available at his or her level or pass the case, along with a written recommendation, to either the court or the parole board, as appropriate.

To ensure that hearings are conducted at or near the place of arrest, within a reasonable period of time, and to reduce travel expenses, five of the hearing officers have separate offices located throughout the state. All hearing officers gather in Columbia for a full day of debriefing and training with the chief hearing officer and the deputy commissioner every two weeks.

Prior to the creation of parole violation guidelines, hearing officers, when finding that probable cause of a violation existed, generally scheduled the offender for a final revocation hearing. The guidelines created an important new function for hearing officers because they were now responsible for determining whether incarceration was in fact necessary, given specific information about the violation's severity and the offender's risk. Hearing officers could choose from a number of alternatives to maintain the offender in the community under supervision. Examples of these are placement in home detention for up to 300 hours, payment of restitution for violations committed during supervision, an increase in the level of supervision or reporting required of the offender, an increase in drug testing, placement in a day reporting center, recommendation for placement in a restitution center, or recommendation for a full or partial revocation.

Cases that have advanced beyond the agent's and hearing officer's level are cases where revocation is appropriate. In parole cases, it remained up to the parole board to determine the length of incarceration required. Prior to the development of violation guidelines, revocations, by agency policy, required offenders to remain incarcerated for one year, after which they would be reconsidered for parole. The guidelines expanded the board's authority to employ any of the options listed for hearing officers or agents and allowed the board to revoke parole and establish a parole release date some time in the future. These alternatives allow the board to fashion an appropriate length of incarceration for offenders who required some period of incarceration.

Benefits of the Parole Violation Process

After experimenting with the parole violation guideline process in some parts of the state, the guidelines were expanded to parole cases statewide in early 1990. A detailed training program was developed and delivered in small groups to all agents to ensure maximum exposure and comprehension. By October 1990, it was clear that these violation guidelines were beneficial for agents, offenders, the department, and the criminal justice community as a whole.

Agents seem pleased with the increased responsibility and the availability of options. The department's clear statements as to expectations concerning violations eased agents' concerns and increased their confidence over violation actions.

Hearing officers are pleased with the expansion of their responsibilities and authority. The department is pleased that offenders who participated in these violation hearings were remaining in the community with increased controls or sanctions in over half of the cases.

The board is pleased that offenders who could be reasonably maintained in the community were remaining under supervision and that this was being done in a way that reduced the number of cases that the board was required to hear. Local jails are enthusiastic about the use of citations instead of warrants, and the Department of Corrections is encouraged by the use of alternative sanctions for violators.

Extending Violation Guidelines to Probation

Expanding violation guidelines to the probation arena involved new challenges for the department because it was not entirely an internal matter. Community sentencing options for probation violators had been a matter within the exclusive control of the court. Several judges were interested in the SCDPPPS violations initiative and supported an experiment to use the guidelines in several counties across the state. Hearing officers were permitted to be as involved in probation violation cases as they were with parole cases. The department specified when hearing officers may impose new conditions or dispose of cases and when they may make recommendations to the court. For instance, an offender who commits several technical violations may be placed under intensive supervision by the hearing officer, but if the violation concerns a special condition imposed by the court or consists of a new crime, the hearing officer would recommend a disposition to the judge, and the court would make the final determination as to the disposition of the case.

Given the greater latitude agents and hearing officers now have in responding to probation violations, they are able to determine the most appropriate response for each violation and each offender. This encourages an active response to violation behavior, which, in turn, encourages offender accountability. Agents have also been pleased at the speed with which cases can be disposed of by hearing officers. At the same time, the courts are being referred only those cases where it is believed that a period of incarceration is warranted or where the court wishes to be involved.

Conclusion

Over half the cases that have passed through the violation process in the parole or probation area have resulted in the offender remaining in the community. The presence of these offenders in the community has not appeared to jeopardize public safety unduly; no apparent increase in the number of new offenses committed by offenders under supervision has occurred during the same time.

There is evidence that the violation practices are having a positive effect on prison crowding. From 1989 to 1990, the department gained nearly 3,000 new offenders to manage, and the number of offenders revoked for technical violations increased by 471. From 1990 to 1991, the department gained over 4,500 new offenders, but experienced essentially no increase in the actual number of offenders on probation or parole who were revoked for technical violations. When the probation violation procedures are expanded from one-third of the probation population to all probationers, an even more dramatic impact is expected.

Judges have generally been agreeable with the recommendations being made. In cases that are referred to the court for disposition, judges are concurring with the recommendations 85 percent of the time. Further, judges are pleased that less of the court's time is spent on probation violation matters. By keeping prosecuting attorneys, public attorneys, sheriffs, and local jailers advised of SCDPPPS actions in these counties, the SCDPPPS has been able to maintain clear lines of communication as to the purpose of its actions, thus strengthening its relationships with different facets of the criminal justice system.

Handling parole and probation violators can be overwhelming. The need to coordinate and consolidate internal agency policies and procedures, establish consistency and proportionality in responding to violations, maintain adequate and accurate information on the outcomes of violation matters, and have confidence in the decision making and internal workings of the violation process are all crucial given the high level of scrutiny that most probation and parole departments face today.

Exchanging vague, misunderstood, and often misapplied discretion in the violations area for a policy-driven, risk-based, cost-effective violations process is a bargain that many probation and parole entities should seek out for themselves. Perhaps the most critical reason for the success of the SCDPPPS effort is that its procedures are based on its desire to improve the way it carries out everyday work. Being neither compelled to achieve a particular result nor required to adopt a specific approach, the SCDPPPS was able to pursue measures that made the most sense. The use of violation guidelines and hearing officers offers probation and parole departments the opportunity to make reasoned, cost-effective decisions regarding offenders under their supervision, while at the same time ensuring the goals and objectives of the department are being met.

Chapter 10

Responding to Probation Violators: The Case of the Cook County Adult Probation Department

By Arthur J. Lurigio, Ph.D.; John J. Robinson, J.D., and Jackie Klosak

Revocations are a necessary but unwelcome aspect of probation operations. When officers revoke high-risk offenders who continue to engage in criminal activity, probation's basic control function is directly served. On the other hand, when officers revoke cases that fail to meet their mandates for treatment or services, the opportunity is lost for offender reintegration or rehabilitation. The violation process is often lengthy and demanding, and probation officers typically can do little to affect the final disposition. With more correctional emphasis on punishment and just deserts, probation agencies are implementing more restrictive programs, and increasing numbers of probation violators are being sent to prison. More effective probation strategies are needed to address these developments.

During the past twenty years, the rate of incarcerations doubled in state and federal institutions (Bureau of Justice Statistics 1990). High percentages of offenders went to prison for long terms and with few hopes for parole because of broad changes in sentencing legislation and a proliferation of strict laws (Irwin & Austin 1987). Policy reforms, such as the abolishment of early release, mandatory minimum sentences, determinate sentencing, and sentencing enhancements, helped to put an unprecedented number of offenders behind bars (Cullen, Clark & Wozniak 1985). At the end of 1989, the nation's prison population reached 703,687 inmates. Its imprisonment rate of approximately 250 per 100,000 people (Bureau of Justice Statistics 1989) presently exceeds that of most European countries (Morris & Tonry 1990). Projections indicate that extensive use of incarceration will continue well into the next century, exacerbating the already severe crowding problem (National Council on Crime and Delinquency 1990).

Institutional Crowding in Illinois

Illinois is one of many states with a prison crowding problem. The precipitous growth of Illinois' prison population can be attributed to two sweeping legal changes occurring in 1978 (Illinois Criminal Justice Information Authority 1989). The first change was the institution of a determinate sentencing structure that resulted

83

in significantly longer prison terms compared with those leveled for the same crimes under the previous indeterminate sentencing structure. In addition, offenders sentenced to "life" became ineligible for release except through executive clemency (Vlasak 1989).

The second change was the creation of a new class of felonies known as class X felonies. Class X felonies include serious crimes, such as aggravated sexual assault, attempted murder, and armed robbery. According to Illinois law, class X felons are not eligible for probation or conditional discharge and must serve their sentences in prison. Since 1978, class 1 felonies, such as residential burglary and aggravated battery of a senior citizen, also carry mandatory prison sentences. These changes led to a substantial increase in the number of Illinois inmates (Vlasak 1989).

To stem the growth of the prison population in Illinois, the state implemented a forced-release program. The program permitted multiple ninety-day increments of meritorious good time that could be applied to inmates' sentences on top of their regular day-for-day good conduct credits. In the three years of the program, 10,000 inmates were released early. In 1983 the Illinois Supreme Court invalidated the practice. According to the Illinois Department of Corrections, this court ruling led to an "overnight population explosion" in Illinois' prison system (Vlasak 1989).

In another attempt to curb its inmate population, the state enacted a law mandating that misdemeanants sentenced to incarceration serve their time in county jails instead of prisons. Despite this effort, the rate of admissions continued to exceed the rate of releases throughout the 1980s, and the prison population kept rising steadily (Illinois Criminal Justice Information Authority 1989). In 1991 the Illinois prison population increased 21 percent over the inmate population in 1989, a growth rate higher than in any other state. In 1992 the difference between actual inmate population and ideal capacity will probably exceed 10,000 (Pearson 1991).

The policy of shunting misdemeanants away from prisons caused a concomitant increase in the jail population, which was also influenced by a surge of drug-related arrests. The problem of jail crowding in Illinois is pronounced in Cook County, where the average daily jail population is higher than that of all the remaining Illinois counties combined (Illinois Department of Corrections 1987). Offenders sent to jail in Cook County have an average stay of 137 days, and more than 500 inmates have been awaiting trial for at least one year. The current jail population is more than 8,000, forcing 1,000 inmates to sleep on the floor. Jail crowding in Cook County was so egregious that a federal judge ordered the county be fined $1,000 for each day the jail exceeded its limit.

Using Probation to Relieve Crowding

During the past decade, criminal justice administrators have relied on routine probation and other community-based sanctions to relieve the crowding problem. Probation is generally considered an effective means to reduce inmate populations and to avoid building new prisons. Nearly two-thirds of convicted adult offenders in the United States are sentenced to probation. It is a sentencing option whose use is growing at the pace of 9,000 new cases each month (Byrne 1987). The probation population has grown faster than the prison, jail, or, parole populations. While the adult prison population increased by 48 percent between 1979 and 1984, the adult probation population increased by 58 percent (Byrne, Lurigio & Baird 1989). During 1990 alone, the number of convicted criminals placed on probation climbed 6 percent to reach a record total of 2.6 million adults on probation by the end of that year (Bureau of Justice Statistics 1991). Table 10-1, adapted from Austin (1990), shows that the probation population more than doubled during the 1980s and that probation is the dominant correctional alternative.

Attention has been given to the rapidly expanding probation population and its affect on correctional practices. Researchers have noted that the push to alleviate institutional crowding has led to probation sentences for serious offenders who pose an immediate threat to public safety (Byrne, Lurigio & Baird 1989). Current caseloads in many jurisdictions comprise high-risk felons who would not have been previously considered for probation. For example, in their seminal report on felony probation in California, Petersilia et al. (1985) revealed that 65 percent of the felony probationers in Los Angeles and Alameda counties were rearrested during probation—many of them for serious offenses, e.g., burglary, assault, and robbery. Furthermore, they found that many felony probationers' conviction offenses and criminal histories were indistinguishable from those of prison inmates. These findings were the first to highlight the downside of using routine probation as the singular alternative to incarceration.

Despite increasing numbers of high-risk offenders, burgeoning caseloads, and climbing recidivism rates, probation budgets have been drastically slashed in many jurisdictions (Lurigio & Petersilia 1992). Jacobs (1987) noted that "the failure to increase [probation] funding in proportion to the increase in caseloads has watered probation down so much that it is widely regarded as providing no punishment or control." For example, over the past ten years, the number of probationers in California has increased 50 percent while the number of probation officers has declined 20 percent. Caseloads have become so large and unmanageable that several departments can render active supervision to only one-third of their cases (Petersilia & Turner 1990). Criminal justice expenditures in many states have been tipped in favor of expanding the prison system at the expense of reducing probation resources (Petersilia 1987).

Table 10-1

The Growth in Correctional Populations (1980–1988)

Type	1980	1988	Increase (%)
Probation	1,118,097	2,356,483	111
Jails	163,994	343,569	110
Prison	329,821	627,588	90
Parole	220,438	407,977	85
Adult Population	162,800,000	128,600,000	12
Adult Arrests	6,100,000	8,500,000	39
Reported Index Crimes	13,400,000	13,900,000	4

Sources: Bureau of Justice Statistics and Federal Bureau of Investigation

The Advent of Intermediate Sanctions

Rampant prison crowding, the exorbitant costs of incarceration, and routine probation's diminished capacity to monitor caseloads of growing size and seriousness eventually led to the development of intermediate sanctions that offer sentencing options beyond the limited choice between probation or prison (Byrne, Lurigio & Petersilia 1992; McCarthy 1987; Morris & Tonry 1990). Intermediate sentences include intensive probation supervision, home confinement, electronic monitoring, boot camps, day centers, monetary penalties, shock probation, and community service.

Although today's intermediate sanctions resemble the "alternatives to incarceration" that emerged in the 1970s, they differ fundamentally in ideology from their counterparts of twenty years ago. Whereas earlier programs were designed to achieve rehabilitation, treatment, and reintegration, contemporary programs are grounded in philosophies of punishment, control, and public safety (Klein-Saffran 1992; Lurigio & Petersilia 1992). These sanctions are touted to accomplish several sweeping objectives: (1) relieve jail and prison crowding, (2) widen the spectrum of sentences, (3) achieve proportionality in sentencing, (4) reduce expenditures through prison diversion, and (5) provide safe and effective community supervision for high-risk offenders.

What affect do these trends have on probation revocations? Prison crowding has necessitated the early release of serious offenders who are often placed on probation as a consequence of parole violations. These offenders, in turn, are likely to fail on probation and end up back in prison. Furthermore, limited prison space has compelled judges to sentence serious offenders to probation in the first place, and such offenders have a greater likelihood of rearrest and revocation.

Byrne and Kelly (1989) estimate that nearly 10 percent of the more than two million offenders on probation in the United States are at "high risk" to recidivate. They also project that 60 percent of these high-risk probationers will be rearraigned within the first year of their sentence. A considerable percentage of new prison and jail admissions are probation violators incarcerated because of technical revocations or new offense convictions (Byrne, Lurigio & Baird 1989). According to the Bureau of Justice Statistics (1988): "Among admissions to prison, conditional release violators made up 5 percent in 1930, 19 percent in 1970, and 23 percent in 1984." Ironically, the increased use of probation has been considered both a primary cause and a primary solution to the prison crowding problem (Byrne, Lurigio & Baird 1989).

Although intermediate sanctions have been heralded as a panacea for institutional crowding (Clear, Flynn & Shapiro 1987), some evidence suggest that they have accelerated crowding through net widening (Clear & Hardyman 1990). Net widening involves sentencing offenders to intermediate penalties when they would have otherwise been placed on routine probation. By definition, the conditions of release on intermediate sanctions (e.g., intensive probation supervision) are more onerous than regular probation and present offenders with more ways to violate, which frequently result in a sentence to jail or prison. Hence, programs purporting to reduce crowding may be inadvertently fostering prison populations by increasing the likelihood of probation violations.

Adult Probation in Cook County

Cook County is the largest county in Illinois, with a current population of more than five million. The county is administered by an elected Board of Commissioners, including a president who is specially elected to preside over this body.

The Circuit Court of Cook County is not only the largest in the state, it is also the largest in the country. The court is divided into the Municipal Department and the County Department, both under the aegis of the chief judge of the Circuit Court.

The Municipal Department is divided into six geographic districts that are further divided into Criminal and Civil Divisions. The First Municipal District (Chicago) also has specialized preliminary hearing courts that concentrate on particular offenses (homicide, auto theft, sexual assault) or on repeat offenders. The Municipal Department generally hears misdemeanor cases or presides over felony preliminary hearings.

The County Department's Criminal Division hears felony cases bound over for trial in Chicago and four suburban locations. The County Department has seven other divisions: chancery, county, domestic relations, juvenile, law, probate, and support. In addition, eight nonjudicial offices are under the auspices of the chief judge: adult probation, pretrial services, jury commissioners, juvenile court services, psychiatric institute, public defender, public guardian, and social services.

The Sentence of Probation

Sentencing laws in Illinois are set forth primarily in Chapter 38 of the *Illinois Revised Statutes*. According to the statutes, there are seven basic sentences that may be leveled alone or in combination: probation, periodic imprisonment, conditional discharge, incarceration, repair of criminal damage to property, fines, and restitution. (Illinois Criminal Justice Information Authority 1989). Consistent with national statistics, probation is the most frequently given sentence in Cook County and in the state of Illinois. From 1977 to 1988, more of Illinois' convicted felons were sentenced to probation than to all other sentences combined. During this period, the number of probation sentences increased 57 percent statewide and 50 percent in Cook County. These increases occurred despite the statutory addition of several new nonprobationable offenses (Illinois Criminal Justice Information Authority 1989).

A sentence of probation cannot be imposed in Illinois for many serious crimes, such as first-degree murder, attempted first-degree murder, and class X felonies (e.g., armed robbery, home invasion, aggravated kidnapping), or for persons judged to be habitual offenders. Probationers are released to the community under mandatory and special conditions and are supervised by sworn probation officers. The maximum length of probation is four years for a class 1 (e.g., attempted armed robbery) or class 2 felony (e.g., burglary), thirty months for a class 3 (e.g., aggravated battery) or class 4 felony (e.g., computer fraud), and one year for a misdemeanor (e.g., retail theft).

The Cook County Adult Probation Department

The Cook County Adult Probation Department is the largest probation agency in the state of Illinois and the fourth largest in the country. Cook County probation officers are employees of the judicial branch of state government and work directly for the Cook County Circuit Court. The Administrative Office of the Illinois Courts-Probation Division helps to develop the county's probation programs. The department is funded partially by the Illinois Supreme Court, which reimburses salaries for probation officers and provides grants for a variety of probation initiatives. In addition to county and state funding, the department collects probation fees for the County Probation Services Fund.

As of 1 September 1992, the department, which was founded in 1911, had a staff of 650, including 479 sworn staff consisting of one chief probation officer, two assistant chief probation officers, twelve deputy chief probation officers, sixty-one probation supervisors, and 403 probation officers. More than 140 personnel work as administrative or support staff. Adult probation facilities are located in Chicago and throughout Cook County at ten separate locations.

The department receives its mandate from § 204-6 Chapter 38 of the *Illinois Revised Statutes*. Its stated mission is to serve the court, protect the community, and support offenders in their efforts to reintegrate successfully into society. Through its traditional probation services, the department conducts presentence investigations, performs risk/needs assessments, refers offenders for services, and monitors mandatory and special conditions of probation. In recent years, the department has significantly broadened the breadth of sentencing options for the court and the range of services for offenders by implementing intensive probation supervision and home confinement programs as well as special programs for mentally ill and drug-abusing probationers.

The department's caseload has risen steeply from 23,000 cases in 1988 to 32,000 in 1992. During this same time period, the average caseload size went from 92 to 108 cases per officer. A recent analysis of department data revealed that 62 percent of the caseload is African-American, 27 percent white, 10 percent Hispanic, and 1 percent Asian, American Indian, or "other." A majority of adult probationers are male (86 percent), and 70 percent are thirty years of age or younger. Furthermore, 84 percent of the department's cases are felonies, 14 percent are misdemeanors, and 2 percent are traffic cases. Since 1983 Cook County's Social Services Agency has assumed responsibility for supervising the bulk of misdemeanor and traffic probations.

Probation Revocations in Cook County

Constitutional and Statutory Rights

Two landmark Supreme Court cases are germane to probation revocations (Nigro 1986). The first case is *Morrissey v. Brewer* (1972) in which the court ruled that parolees are entitled to preliminary and final parole revocation hearings. The court stipulated that the final hearing must be convened within a reasonable time after the parolee is taken into custody. The court held further that the parolee must be accorded at the hearing minimum due process rights, such as the right to be heard in person, present witnesses and documentary evidence, and confront and cross-examine adverse witnesses.

The second case is *Gagnon v. Scarpelli* (1973) in which the court ruled that there is no difference between parole and probation revocation with respect to due process rights. Moreover, the court decided that the minimum requirements of due process also included the right to receive written notice of the alleged violation of probation. Similarly, an Illinois appellate court held that a probationer must receive sufficient notice concerning the alleged conduct that prompted the revocation proceedings. However, such notice need not have the same degree of detail demanded of an indictment (*People v. White* 1975). In *People v. Crawford* (1980), the Illinois appellate court ruled that the state may be precluded from filing a petition for violation of probation if it waits an unreasonably long period of time to do so.

The *Illinois Revised Statute*, Chapter 38, § 1005-6-4(c), specifies that the state has the burden of proving the violation of probation by a preponderance of evidence and that the probationer has the statutory rights of confrontation, cross-examination, and representation by counsel. The statute also calls for the court to retain discretion to recommit the probation violator to the original probation, with or without modifying the conditions, or to sentence the probation violator to any other sentence available at the time of the initial sentence. In regard to resentencing, the statute § 1005-6-4(h) indicates that time on probation shall not be credited by the court against a sentence of imprisonment or periodic imprisonment unless the court orders otherwise.

Revocation Policy

The Cook County Adult Probation Department's policy on violations of probation was written to conform with American Correctional Association standards. The policy reads as follows (Cook County Adult Probation 1991):

> Supervising officers shall adhere to all established monitoring procedures and shall attempt to resolve non-compliance issues internally to avoid the initiation of administrative violations of probation. Violations of probation for new criminal behavior shall be investigated promptly by the supervising officer and reported to the court by requesting a petition for violation of probation. Staff representing the department at court proceedings pertaining to probation matters shall provide the court with accurate, factual information. All information provided to the court both verbally and in writing shall be clear, concise, well-organized and in established formats. Officers shall advise the court of case progress or lack thereof through status reports, and shall present formal opinions to clarify and amend court orders.

Revocation Procedures

Chapter 38 of the *Illinois Revised Statute*, § 1005-6-3(a), dictates five mandatory conditions of probation. The probationer shall (1) not violate any criminal statute of any jurisdiction, (2) report to or appear in person before such person or agency as directed by the court, (3) refrain from possessing a firearm or other dangerous weapon, (4) not leave the state without permission of the court, and (5) permit the probation officer to visit him or her at home or elsewhere to the extent necessary to discharge the probation officer's duties. In addition, the statute allows the court discretion to set special conditions of probation relating to the nature of the offense or the rehabilitation of the offender.

A probation officer's case reports must reflect the probationer's compliance with the conditions of probation. If a probationer has not complied with any of these conditions, the supervising officer must specifically indicate the failure to comply in a petition charging the offender with a violation of probation. According to department policy, a probation officer must summarily institute a violation-of-probation petition when an offender has committed a subsequent crime or has been found in possession of a firearm or any other dangerous weapon. The probation officer must prepare case file documentation of these occurrences. When a probationer has failed to maintain contact with his or her probation officer for thirty days, the officer should proceed as follows:

1. Contact the probationer by telephone to inform him or her of the failure to comply with reporting standards.
2. Send a delinquent letter directing the probationer to report at a specified date and time.
3. Contact by telephone or mail those personal references given by the probationer to ascertain or verify his or her whereabouts.
4. Make a home visit to the probationer after receiving supervisory approval.

If the officer cannot contact an offender for sixty days, he or she must prepare a violation-of-probation petition and must initiate the following procedure to launch a violation-of-probation hearing:

1. The probation officer prepares a complete, up-to-date record sheet reflecting all information concerning the probationer's failure to comply with the conditions of probation, including documentation of arrest reports and criminal histories, case materials, ledger sheets, and resource agency letters.
2. The probation officer fills out a request for the typing of court documents relating to revocations.
3. The probation officer submits to his or her supervisor all violation-of-probation (VOP) forms and documentation for discussion and review.
4. Support staff prepare the VOP petition for court and set a court date for the VOP hearing.
5. The probation officer reviews and signs the VOP petition and submits it to his or her supervisor for review.
6. The probation officer compiles VOP materials and prepares for the revocation hearing.

Cook County Revocation Statistics

Cook County revocation data were collected by Cunniff and Shilton (1991) in a national study of felony probationers, which included samples of cases from thirty-two jurisdictions across sixteen states. The investigators analyzed case information from a cohort of Cook County adult offenders sentenced to probation in 1986. Results showed that 41 percent of these offenders had been involved in at least one VOP hearing. The precipitating factors that led to the hearings varied considerably: 39 percent were for technical violations, 36 percent were for new arrests, 23 percent were for abscondings, and 2 percent were for new convictions or miscellaneous infractions. More recent Cook County statistics revealed that in 1989 a significantly greater percentage of revocations (67 percent) were filed because of technical violations.

After the 1986 cohort had been on probation for nearly three years, Cunniff and Shilton (1991) reported that 52 percent had successfully completed their probation, 28 percent were still on probation, 10 percent had absconded, 9 percent had their probation revoked, and 1 percent exited their probation for other reasons (e.g., death). Compared with other jurisdictions in the investigation, Cook County's rate of successful completions was significantly higher than the overall average of 32 percent, and its rate of revocations was significantly lower than the overall average of 22 percent. The department had the fifth highest rate of successful completions and the fifth lowest rate of revocations.

In an earlier Cook County study on recidivism, Lurigio (1986) examined 500 felony cases sentenced to adult probation during a five-year interval (1979–1983). The primary purpose of the research was to identify predictors of rearrest. Findings demonstrated that a majority of probationers were revoked because of rearrest (70 percent) or absconding (23 percent). Only 7 percent of the revocations were because of technical violations. These results are dramatically different from Cook County revocation statistics for 1989 and from the results of the Cunniff and Shilton (1991) study, both of which showed that a much higher percentage of Cook County revocations were the results of technical violations.

Lurigio (1986) also reported that more than half (55 percent) of the violations in Cook County led to recommitment to probation, often with an extension of the felon's current sentence, while 22 percent of the new arrest revocations led to a jail or prison term. Both Lurigio (1986) and Cunniff and Shilton (1991) found that age, gender, employment, prior record, and drug use were significantly related to revocation. Specifically, offenders who are young, male, unemployed, and who have criminal histories and drug abuse problems are typically poorer risks on probation.

Conclusions and Recommendations

As the data suggest, the proportion of technical violations in Cook County has grown precipitously during the past decade. The growth may be partially explained by the addition of special probation programs, such as intensive probation supervision and home confinement, which contain more stringent conditions of release and therefore spur the rate of technical violations. This unbidden consequence of intermediate sanctions does not necessarily call for a diminution in their use or a moratorium on their further development and implementation.

Instead, it should prompt consideration of more innovative strategies for utilizing those sentencing alternatives to handle probation revocations. Technical violations are generally viewed as less serious than new arrest revocations. Nevertheless, they involve comparable levels of preparation, paperwork, and court time and impose a considerable strain on probation and court resources. Probation departments should be given the discretion to punish or control technical violators without court involvement. In the model, agencies would have the court's or statute's authority to move offenders "up and down" a continuum of sanctions in response to their performance on the current sentence. For example, offenders on intensive probation supervision who violate curfew or any other administrative or ministerial condition of their probation may be placed on home confinement (with or without electronic monitoring) in lieu of or as an addendum to the existing conditions of intensive probation supervision. To date, most jurisdictions only permit "downward" movement, such as gradually slackening the rules of release as offenders pass successfully through the various stages of an intermediate punishment program until they are finally placed on routine probation.

Overall, to become more adaptable to current probation caseloads and sentencing practices, departments must look to more flexible policies and procedures for addressing the problem of revocations.

References

Austin, J. 1990. *America's growing correctional-industrial complex.* Madison, Wis.: National Council on Crime and Delinquency.

Bureau of Justice Statistics. 1988. Prisoners in 1987. *BJS Bulletin.*

Bureau of Justice Statistics. 1989. Prisoners in 1988. *BJS Bulletin.*

Bureau of Justice Statistics. 1990. *Prisons.* Washington, D.C.: U.S. Department of Justice.

Bureau of Justice Statistics. 1991. *Probation and parole 1990.* Washington, D.C.: U.S. Department of Justice.

Byrne, J. M. 1992. Are intermediate sanctions really effective? A review of the evidence. In *Smart sentencing: The emergence of intermediate sanctions,* ed. J. M. Byrne, A. J. Lurigio, and J. Petersilia. Newbury Park, Calif.: Sage.

Byrne, J. M. 1987. *Probation.* Washington, D.C.: National Institute of Justice.

Byrne, J. M., A. J. Lurigio, and J. Petersilia. 1992. *Smart sentencing: The emergence of intermediate sanctions.* Newbury Park, Calif.: Sage.

Byrne, J. M., A. J. Lurigio, and S. C. Baird. 1989. The effectiveness of the new intensive supervision programs. *Research in Corrections* 2: 1–48.

Byrne, J. M., and L. Kelly. 1989. *Restructuring probation as an intermediate sanction: An evaluation of the Massachusetts Intensive Probation Supervision program.* Washington, D.C.: National Institute of Justice.

Clear, T. R., and P. L. Hardyman. 1990. The new intensive supervision movement. *Crime and Delinquency* 36: 42–61.

Clear, T. R., S. Flynn, and C. Shapiro. 1987. Intensive supervision in probation: A comparison of three projects. In *Intermediate punishments: Intensive supervision, home confinement, and electronic surveillance,* ed. B. R. McCarthy. Monsey, N.Y.: Criminal Justice Press.

Cook County Adult Probation Department. 1991. *Cook County Adult Probation Department: Policy and procedure manual.* Chicago: Cook County Adult Probation Department.

Cullen, F. T., G. A. Clark, and J. F. Wozniak. 1985. Explaining the get tough movement: Can the public be blamed? *Federal Probation* 49: 16–24.

Cunniff, Illinois Criminal Justice Information Authority. 1989. *Trends and issues 1989: Criminal and juvenile justice in Illinois.* Chicago: Illinois Criminal Justice Information Authority.

Illinois Department of Corrections. 1987. *Fiscal year 1987 jail and detention statistics and information.* Springfield, Ill.: Illinois Department of Corrections.

Irwin, J., and J. Austin. 1987. *It's about time: Solving America's prison crowding problem.* San Francisco: National Council on Crime and Delinquency.

Jacobs, J. B. 1987. *Inside prisons.* Washington, D.C.: National Institute of Justice.

Klein-Saffran, J. 1992. The impact of intermediate punishments of the federal corrections system. In *Smart sentencing: The emergence of intermediate sanctions,* ed. J. M. Byrne, A. J. Lurigio, and J. Petersilia. Newbury Park, Calif.: Sage.

Lurigio, A. J. 1986. *Describing and predicting recidivism among felony probationers: A limited replication of the RAND study.* Case classification research project: Report no. 6. Chicago: Cook County Adult Probation Department.

Lurigio, A. J., and J. Petersilia. 1992. The emergence of intensive probation supervision (IPS) programs in the United States. In *Smart sentencing: The emergence of intermediate sanctions,* ed. J. M. Byrne, A. J. Lurigio, and J. Petersilia. Newbury Park, Calif.: Sage.

McCarthy, B. R., ed. 1987. *Intermediate punishments: Intensive supervision, home confinement, and electronic surveillance.* Monsey, N.Y.: Criminal Justice Press.

Morris, N., and M. Tonry. 1990. *Between prison and probation: Intermediate punishments in a rational sentencing system.* New York: Oxford University Press.

National Council on Crime and Delinquency. 1990. *Intensive supervision in the United States: A review of recent experience and critical issues with recommendations for future development.* Madison, Wis.: National Council on Crime and Delinquency.

Nigro, J. B. 1986. Probation revocation. In *Prosecution of the criminal case manual.* Chicago: Illinois Institute of Continuing Legal Education.

Pearson, R. 1991. "State prison population is surging." *Chicago Tribune* (6 October): 6.

Petersilia, J. 1987. *Expanding options for criminal sentencing.* Santa Monica, Calif.: RAND Corporation.

Petersilia, J., and S. Turner. 1990. *Intensive supervision for high-risk probationers: Findings from three California experiments.* Santa Monica, Calif.: RAND Corporation.

Petersilia, J., et al. 1985. *Granting felons probation: Public risks and alternatives.* Santa Monica, Calif.: RAND Corporation.

Vlasak, T. 1989. A bad problem gets worse. *The Compiler* 9: 11–13

Chapter 11

The Expanded Use of Intermediate Sanctions in Morris County, New Jersey

By Jude Del Preore

The Probation Services Division in Morris County, New Jersey, which has juris-diction over thirty-nine towns and cities, is organized into several subunits: adult supervision and field services, juvenile supervision, support enforcement, and spe-cial services. There is also an administrative unit, which encompasses budget, finance and procurement, management information systems, branch operations, clerical support, and special projects.

The Adult Supervision and Field Services Section monitors offenders placed under supervision by the court. Offenders have the opportunity to prove them-selves under the guidance of a court-appointed probation officer, who helps im-plement court orders and special conditions specified by the court while identifying and resolving problem areas in the probationer's life. Some examples of frequently imposed court sanctions are drug testing, community service, fines, restitution, and financial penalties. Probation Services has initiated Project FORCE (Financial Obligation Recovery and Collection Effort) to enhance collec-tion of court-imposed financial obligations. Probation officers also supervise of-fenders on orders from out-of-county and out-of-state courts.

The Community Service Program of Morris County Probation was initiated in 1982 in response to a directive from the New Jersey State Legislature. The pro-gram provides a positive alternative to traditional sentencing. According to New Jersey state law, a judge may sentence offenders to perform unpaid community service in lieu of incarceration. This may be completed as a condition of probation or as a requirement of a conditional discharge. The sentencing judge sets the num-ber of hours to be worked, and the offender is required to perform a minimum number of hours weekly.

Current Violation Policy and Procedures

It is the policy of the Adult Supervision and Field Services Section that standard and special conditions of probation imposed by the court be effectively enforced for the protection of the community.

The legal basis for violation-of-probation proceedings is provided by New Jer-sey Criminal Code Title 2C:45-3. At any time before the discharge of the defen-dant or the termination of the period of suspension or probation, the court and/or the Probation Services Division may intervene to either revoke probation or arrest. It is also the court's prerogative to hand down a new sentence. Although probation officers may not ultimately be seeking a revocation of probation when a violation-of-probation charge is filed, the charge is tantamount to asking for revocation. Officers are encouraged to make the court aware of their recommendations in regard to continuing the term of probation or not.

When the offender willfully refuses to pay fines, restitutions, etc., a violation of probation will be charged. The probation officer also has the authority to charge the offender with a technical violation of probation, which refers to the fact that the probationer has inexcusably failed to comply with a substantial requirement imposed as a condition of probation.

A charge of violation of probation may also be filed if the probation officer has probable cause to believe that the probationer has committed a subsequent offense. In rare occasions involving a direct threat to public welfare, a charge of violation of probation can be filed. According to New Jersey law, the defendant does not have to be arrested for a new offense before a charge of violation of probation is filed. The probation officer having probable cause to believe that a new offense has been committed has substantial grounds to file a violation of probation charge.

Probation officers have a certain amount of discretion as to when to file a charge of violation of probation. In situations involving a technical violation of probation, it is wise to document that a series of progressive warnings has been issued to the offender, but the officer should not allow technical violations to continue over a long period of time without a charge being filed. For example, probation officers are instructed not to wait until two weeks before the term of probation expires to file violation of probation charges based on failure to pay, failure to attend counseling, and so forth.

Probation officers also have discretion on whether to file a violation of probation charge for a new offense. In general, officers need not charge a probationer with violation of probation based on subsequent misdemeanors, unless that offense resulted in injury to a victim.

Probation officers have the authority to arrest a probationer, which calls for a high degree of professional discretion. Because probation officials in New Jersey are unarmed, some maintain that they should not try to arrest an individual without support from local law enforcement officials. In addition, the probation officer may need to contact a judge or chief probation officer for formal commitment of the probationer to the county jail. A proper notice of violation of probation should be served on the probationer as soon as possible after his or her arrest.

The Morris County Probation Services Division uses urine monitoring as a condition of supervision to deter drug use by probationers. Primary urine monitoring is also used as a tool for offender management. It helps probationers recognize a substance abuse problem and leads to referral to an appropriate treatment facility. Thus, the primary urine testing policy is aimed at the rehabilitation of the probationer.

Secondary, or confirmatory, urine testing is used to confirm presumptive primary positive test results for the purpose of prosecution. Confirmatory testing almost always involves chain-of-custody handling and gas chromatography/mass spectrometry testing. The probation officer has the right to refuse any urine sample submitted under circumstances where the probation officer has any doubt regarding sample integrity. In any case where a sample is refused by the probation officer, an effort shall be made immediately to closely monitor the collection of a second sample.

The minimum testing frequency is once randomly (i.e., not scheduled, but at an unpredictable time) per month for the first six months of supervision. This applies to all offenders for whom drug testing was court ordered. This policy is the minimum standard requirement for court-ordered drug testing and does not preclude officers from testing more frequently or testing also on scheduled appointments. Special attention is given to offenders with a history of violence, current or recent drug use, community or familial reports of drug involvement, etc. In such cases, officers are expected to increase the frequency of testing. If a sample comes up positive at any stage, the standard of testing is to begin over again within the initial classification with a warning that a second positive urine result will be reported to the court. In all cases when the offender disputes the positive urine result, it is sent for further testing.

Trend Analysis

The incarceration rate in Morris County has risen substantially since 1984, increasing from 0.40 per 1,000 population to 0.70 per 1,000 in 1989—a 75 percent increase. Both number of admissions and length of stay have maintained fairly steady growth rates and are reflected in the dramatic increase in the average daily population figures. The inmate capacity of the Morris County Jail as established by the New Jersey Department of Corrections is 144. However, the average daily population from 1984 to 1989 was 236—164 percent of capacity. Average monthly population for 1990 indicates average admissions of 303, with an average length of stay fluctuating between twenty-three and twenty-nine days.

The aggregate adult probation caseload between 1985 and 1990 has risen by 89 percent. There has been a six-year growth trend in caseloads from a yearly average of 1,749 cases in 1985 to 3,300 in 1990.

During 1990, probation officers of the Adult Supervision and Field Services Section issued 206 violations of probation, 37 of which resulted in terms of incarceration, 21 in remands to the Morris County Jail, 2 in remands to the Morris County Jail only on weekends, 3 in sentences to a state correctional facility, 1 in a sentence to the Morris County labor farm, and 4 in admittance to the Morris County Sheriff's Labor Assistance Program (SLAP). Six received credit for time served.

It is important to note that in 1990 the median of inmate incarceration as the result of a violation of probation, for any given month, was seven. These seven inmates represented 2 percent of the overall jail population. Given the problem of crowding at the jail, it is clear that judges are being forced to examine and use alternative intermediate sanctions.

Dispositional Enforcement

Rigorous enforcement of community-based judicial dispositions is critical to their success. The effectiveness of conditional sentences that require the fulfillment of release conditions, such as payment of financial sanctions, community service, and treatment, depends on recognition by the offender that courts will take the steps necessary to ensure compliance. Effective enforcement techniques will make offenders perceive the necessity of meeting the conditions of community release and will enable enforcement agents to see that the orders are fulfilled.

In this regard, it has become increasingly difficult to enforce judicial dispositions in New Jersey because of an increase in mandatory penalties, an increase in the number of offenders being sentenced, procedural requirements having increased court staff demands, pretrial processing matters taking priority for court time, and inadequately equipped courts and court support operations (space, equipment, and technology).

Additionally, probation services (the enforcement arm of the court in New Jersey) has seen its responsibilities and workload increase dramatically, and probation resources have not kept pace with its workload growth. These conditions have reduced Probation Service's ability to effectively enforce the financial and community service obligations imposed by the court. This growing trend has become a major concern for judges, probation officers, court administrators, prosecutors, victims, and the public.

The public believes that the court system is not effectively discharging its responsibility to hold offenders accountable. New Jersey's jails are seriously crowded. Offenders realize that it is unlikely that they will be incarcerated for failure to comply with court-ordered obligations. A general lack of progressively intensive sanctions short of incarceration contributes to the impression that offenders may disregard court orders.

These factors cause frustration among judges, probation officers, prosecutors, wardens, sheriffs, victims, and the public. To ameliorate these problems, Morris County developed a new and effective enforcement approach, one that provides a flexible range of viable options short of incarceration designed to hold offenders accountable. This cooperative approach was designed to achieve the following goals:

- ease jail crowding
- hold offenders accountable for meeting court-imposed requirements
- increase rates of compliance for the payments of fines, restitution, financial penalties, and community service
- establish a range of graduated community-based sanctions for offenders who fail to comply
- establish a partnership between the judiciary, the executive branch agencies, and the community to administer program elements

The cooperative approach will do the following:

- ease jail crowding
- improve community service and fine payment compliance rates
- save money
- require few resources
- be easy to implement
- improve intergovernmental coordination
- enhance rehabilitative efforts
- reduce indirect costs
- restore credibility and foster confidence by the public in the courts

Intermediate Sanctions

An intermediate sanction refers to any type of corrective intervention that may vary in level of intensity and restrictiveness of control or treatment. The focus of this intervention may be punitive, rehabilitative, or supervision-oriented. In the adult system in Morris county, the primary concern has been developing mid-level punitive responses that can help avoid unnecessary incarceration.

Currently, the Morris County Probation Services Division, the Morris County Sheriff's Office, and the court have implemented many initiatives in the area of intermediate sanctions to address the concern of jail crowding.

Sanctions used by the courts in Morris County include jail tours, community service, placement in the Sheriff's Labor Assistance Program (SLAP), and house curfews. All four provide sentencing alternatives that rely on resources provided by Probation Services and the Sheriff's Office.

The use of intermediate sanctions underscores the need for professional, well-trained officers to provide successful alternatives to the court. There is a need for an even broader-based group of intermediate sanctions involving both the Sheriff's Office and local municipalities.

The following sanctions are presently used in Morris County.

House Curfew

As part of a condition of probation or sanction for the violation of probation, the judge may order house curfew. House curfew is a set time designated by court order that the probationers must be confined to their place of residence. Either the probationer must contact the officer or the officer must initiate contact on entering the residence. This sanction is currently used rather extensively in the supervision of juveniles.

Jail Tours

Jails tours are used by the court to impress on the probationer that incarceration may be the result of violating probation conditions. It is more of an educational tool or reality therapy than a punitive measure. Many judges use jail tours as a standard measure in their sentencing for juvenile offenders and in pretrial supervision cases.

Sheriff's Labor Assistance Program

The Sheriff's Labor Assistance Program (SLAP) allows convicted offenders and probationers the opportunity to "work off" their sentence rather than spend time in jail. All probationers live outside the county correctional facilities and work in the program on weekends. Their duties vary from working on the Sheriff's Office farm to helping rebuild dilapidated parts of town (group community service sites). This program is open to low-risk offenders only. The one standard rule is that if program participants are absent on their assigned day, they are taken out of the program and incarcerated.

Community Service

Community service by offenders is being used as a sentencing alternative with increasing frequency. Offenders sentenced to community service work without monetary compensation at public or private nonprofit agencies in the community.

These offenders usually perform their community service during the evenings and on weekends to complete their sentences. The punitive aspect of a community service order is reflected in the imposition on the time and freedom of offenders. While functioning in the traditional role as punishment, a community service order also directly benefits the public through the performance of services that may otherwise not be available.

As a community-based sentence, a community service order is relatively inexpensive compared with the costs of other penalties, such as incarceration. With increasing jail crowding and budgetary limitations, community service offers the courts and the public a viable, cost-effective means of punishment.

The community service program of Morris County was initiated in 1982 in response to a directive from the New Jersey state legislature. The program provides a positive alternative to traditional sentencing.

According to New Jersey law, a judge may sentence offenders to perform unpaid community service in lieu of incarceration. After an evaluation of such criteria as previous criminal history and severity of crime, eligible offenders are recommended to this alternative sentencing program. This intermediate sanction may be completed as a conditional discharge. A majority of participants have been ordered to donate their time as the result of a conviction for driving while intoxicated.

Electronic Monitoring Program

The electronic monitoring (EM) program is an alternative to institutional incarceration available to certain offenders, both presentenced and sentenced. The program is aimed at offenders who require less than facility custody but more than probation supervision.

The Sheriff's Office instituted this program as a form of house arrest. In the past few years, EM programs have become a significant means of punishing offenders. EM programs limit offenders' external activities and yet save money and jail space by allowing the incarcerated defendant to be released from jail but confined to home except while at work or participating in other authorized activities, such as SLAP or community-based treatment programs. Participants are required to pay a user's fee for this service.

High-intensity Probation

The Morris County Probation Services Division implemented a high-impact probation (HIP) unit. As many as thirty defendants receive intense supervision and maximal rehabilitative services, offering the greatest protection to the community and ensuring a rapid return to court for those who continue to violate probation conditions.

The HIP program is designed for high-risk probationers who have failed to comply with probation under standard supervision and who have been assessed on intake as presenting a high degree of risk of failure on probation. It provides an intermediate, noncustodial alternative for probation violators, freeing jail space for those truly in need of incarceration.

HIP offers a realistic incentive to cooperate with probation under standard supervision, making standard supervision more meaningful, providing better protection to the community, and facilitating a rapid return to court for those who continue to violate probation under HIP supervision. It also includes intensive supervision mandating frequent face-to-face contact and curfew checks by an experienced probation officer.

Programmatic requirements include regular random urine monitoring and, in many instances, abstinence from alcohol. Gainful employment is another condition of HIP supervision, as is frequent verification with special conditions, such as counseling, community service, SLAP, and monetary obligations.

Probation officers maintain ongoing contact with family members and significant others to assist in monitoring offenders' compliance. Electronic surveillance may be incorporated to monitor curfew compliance.

Centralized Enforcement Court

At one time, intermediate sanctions were being implemented by various agencies within the Morris County criminal justice community. Such sanctions have been imposed by the thirty-nine municipal courts and eight different superior court judges sitting in Morris County. This resulted in the system being fragmented and in need of more coordination.

In the past two years, the county has taken measures to create a comprehensive enforcement network by channeling all violations of court orders to one judge in the Superior Court.

This integrated enforcement hearing by the same judge immediately produced positive results. A consistent sanctioning policy for sentence violators went into effect, a unified bench warrant process was instituted, and all other sentencing problems were dealt with at one hearing. Within a few weeks SLAP attendance tripled, fines were being paid, compliance with community service work requirements increased, and credibility began to be given to the court enforcing its own orders. A unified, integrated enforcement procedure that used intermediate sanctions grew as the primary form of punishment.

Conclusion

Prison crowding in the United States vis-a-vis Morris County, New Jersey, has reached crisis proportions. One response has been to expand prison capacity. However, prison construction is expensive and, in times of budgetary constraints, can drain resources from other important programs.

There is a definite need for more jail space to accommodate offenders who fail in the traditional probation supervision mode. Because of the lack of space, few offenders who violate the conditions of probation receive a sentence of incarceration, either pre- or postdisposition. In fact, on a total mean probation caseload of 3,300, only seven individuals (annualized) were incarcerated at any one time during 1990. Because of this, Morris County has been prompted to experiment with programmatic alternatives to incarceration—intermediate sanctions.

Jail crowding has affected traditional probation. However, it has also served as a creative impetus to find meaningful alternatives. Although the alternative programs described cost more to implement than traditional probation, they are still less expensive than incarceration.

Chapter 12

Intermediate Sanctions and Violations Policy in Probation and Parole: Prescriptions for the 1990s

By Edward E. Rhine and Kermit Humphries

During the past decade, the probation and parole population in nearly every juris-diction in the country grew dramatically. According to a recent Bureau of Justice Statistics (1991) report, between 1985 and 1990 the number of offenders on probation increased nearly 36 percent, from 1,968,712 to 2,670,234. The number of those on parole rose 77 percent, from 300,203 to 531,407. Within this same period, the prison population grew 77 percent to over 745,000. This growth has been accompanied by an increase in the total number of offenders whose proba-tion or parole status has been revoked.

To what extent are probation and parole revocation practices fueling prison population growth? As Dale Parent notes in "Structuring Policies to Address Sanctions for Absconders and Violators," in some states two-thirds of offenders are admitted to prison because they have had their probation or parole status revoked; the remaining third are newly sentenced admissions. Clearly, shifts in revocation policy—either by the courts or by paroling authorities—can sig-nificantly affect a jurisdiction's prison and jail population.

Many states have developed and implemented intermediate sanctions to ad-dress probation and parole violators. These sanctions provide an alternative short of doing nothing or of returning the violator to prison. Such sanctions may include intensive supervision programs, house arrest, electronic monitoring, community service, day reporting centers, and short-term confinement units. These sanctions may be, and often are, used in tandem to enhance the effectiveness of supervision. Many jurisdictions have moved quickly to adopt an array of intermediate sanc-tions. This trend—which will continue to accelerate during the next decade and beyond—holds significant promise for probation and parole. However, this promise will be achieved only if such sanctions are properly designed and fully in-tegrated as a matter of policy into a jurisdiction's approach to supervision case management.

The recommendations that follow address a number of key issues that policy makers and program administrators should consider in relation to using inter-mediate sanctions with probation and parole violators. Although the recommenda-tions are not exhaustive in their focus, they offer sensible prescriptions for moving away from the tendency to rely too heavily on revocation as the preferred ap-proach to dealing with those who violate the conditions of supervision.

Structuring Responses According to Agency Policy

Community supervision is generally designed to help probationers and parolees, control their activities, and monitor their compliance with the conditions established by the judge or the parole board. These conditions—both general and specific—are designed to reduce the likelihood of new criminal behavior. Thus movement and travel may be limited, association with known felons prohibited, and the use of alcohol or drugs explicitly forbidden. Special conditions may be added if programmatic intervention is required or certain behavior needs to be deterred.

In many jurisdictions how an agency responds to rules violation, especially technical violations, is generally unstructured. The high degree of discretion that exists results in inconsistent responses to violations by probationers and parolees. In most states, formal guidance to line officers, especially when dealing with technical violators, is either nonexistent, haphazard, or subject to the constraints of prison and jail crowding.

Depending on the jurisdiction, the responsibility for developing violations policy resides with the parole board, parole field services, and the judiciary or the probation department. This responsibility may be shared across agencies or even across branches of government, especially when dealing with probationers. Clearly, the lack of a coherent policy framework for responding to probation and parole violators carries significant consequences. The absence of explicit policy leaves line officers confused, undermines agency morale, and weakens the effectiveness of supervision.

Formal policy in this area should express the agency's rationale for responding to major and minor violations of the rules. It should explain to field personnel why a course of action should be taken and the general parameters within which they must operate. Just as important, the framing of such policy illustrates that revocation is only one of several options that probation and parole officials may take when confronted with offender noncompliance.

As a critical first step in creating or revising existing policy, it is essential that revocation be viewed as but a subset of overall violations policy. Within this context, the objectives to be served when addressing violation behavior should be clearly defined. Likewise, an agency's policy should describe the types of actions to be taken at specific junctures in the violations process. To the extent that this occurs, the agency's violations policy will contribute to a more rational, fair, and consistent response to probationer and parolee noncompliance.

Some jurisdictions have begun to structure policy in this area. As discussed by Richard Stroker, in 1988 the South Carolina Department of Probation, Parole, and Pardon Services began a technical assistance project under the auspices of the National Institute of Corrections to consider its handling of parole violators. At the time, no overriding philosophy governed the department's approach to violations policy. If a violation occurred, officers in the field were expected to respond. However, there was no specific guidance on what constituted an appropriate response.

During the course of the project the department piloted revocation guidelines that prescribed specific responses for clearly defined types of violations. The policy separated violation behavior into categories and defined the range of responses appropriate to the various possible violations. The policy also indicated what responses might be taken, within prescribed limits, by parole officers, parole supervisors, hearing officers, and the parole board. In 1990 the parole violations guidelines were expanded to include probation.

The South Carolina project involved an enormous investment in staff time and agency resources. Nonetheless, the success of this undertaking provided a number of tangible benefits not the least of which was to clearly convey to field personnel the parole board's expectations regarding the most appropriate response given the seriousness of the violation and the risk posed by the offender. Confusion was sharply reduced, offender accountability was increased, and those who warranted revocation as a result of the seriousness of the violation were returned to custody.

Violations Policy and Supervision Case Management

During the 1980s, the National Institute of Corrections sponsored what has since become known as the Model Probation/Parole Classification and Case Management Project. The model that was disseminated included four basic components: the use of an instrument-based risk and needs assessment, the adoption of client management classification to assist in case planning, the use of a management information system, and the deployment of a workload versus a caseload system for assigning offenders and investigations. The project's influence has been most notable with respect to the classification of offenders based on a formal assessment of risks and needs (Burke et al. 1990).

In most jurisdictions, classifying offenders using risk and needs assessments is now common. A system of classification is a tool to enhance supervision case management. Many agencies have carefully considered their supervision levels, the contact standards associated with each level, and how to achieve the objectives of supervision through formal case planning.

What is often overlooked, however, is the linkage between supervision case management and responses to probation and parole violators. The act of revocation represents only one component within the much broader framework of an agency's violations policy. Yet, violations policy itself is shaped by and given coherence only within the parameters of the goals established by an agency's philosophy of supervision. These goals may emphasize public safety and control, treatment and rehabilitation of the offender, deterrence, incapacitation, or some combination. Which of these goals are paramount, or how they are to be balanced, will establish the broad parameters within which violations policy will be carried out.

There remains the tendency to view the violations response, especially revocation of probation or parole, as the final step an agency takes when an offender fails to comply with the rules. The careful crafting and implementation of an agency's approach to offender classification and case management is often done apart from a consideration of how violations policy might, in fact, assist in achieving the goals of supervision. Properly conceived violations policy represents an integral component of an effective system of case management. However, the integration of one with the other requires a clear distinction between offender behavior that warrants revocation and that which does not.

Numerous studies have concluded that convicted felons under community supervision are high-risk and recidivism-prone. However, a closer look at some of these studies suggests that the frequency and meaning of offender recidivism is not self-evident. To the extent that such studies treat the failure rates of offenders as synonymous with recidivism, they contribute to the perception that a vast majority of violations by probationers and parolees warrant revocation. Policy makers must distinguish clearly between recidivism (i.e., new criminal acts) and violations by offenders that may amount to noncompliance, but not criminal behavior.

A 1984 Bureau of Justice Statistics report examined how parolees released from fourteen states fared during a three-year period. The results indicated that 32 percent of the sample were returned to custody within this time frame. Technical violations may have composed as many as half of those in the releasee cohort.

A more recent survey by Herrick (1989) reported on the findings from forty-six states, which together had 365,823 offenders on parole in 1987. Of these, 78,000 or 21 percent had their parole revoked. Of this, 42 percent were revoked for committing a new crime; 55 percent for technical violations. The reasons most frequently given for revoking parole, excluding new criminal involvement, included failing to participate in a stipulated treatment program, leaving an assigned area without permission, failing to report to a parole officer, abusing alcohol or drugs, and failing to secure or hold employment.

Although these statistics refer to parolees, they illustrate the importance of clearly distinguishing which violations warrant revocation and which do not.

Regardless of the nature of the infraction, the appropriate response should be structured through agency policy. Major violations should be distinguished from minor or chronic technical violations. The differential response to the severity of the violation, if defined through policy, will contribute to consistency, proportionality, and fairness when dealing with offenders.

A significant percentage of probationers and parolees will violate the rules during their term of supervision. The frequency and seriousness of such violations will vary considerably. In some cases, violations of the rules may indicate that the offender is experiencing problems that will become even more pronounced unless addressed through timely and effective case management. In such instances, the response to violations is not just a matter of imposing punitive sanctions on offenders. Rather, as Dale Parent says in his chapter, the response to violations should be viewed as an integral component of effective case management. Holding probationers and parolees accountable for their behavior, but using noncompliance as an opportunity for ameliorative intervention, suggests the direct and vital linkage between supervision case management and an agency's approach to violations policy.

Defining the Rationale and Use of Intermediate Sanctions

To date, most of the discussion of intermediate sanctions has centered on their use as a sentencing option that falls on a continuum between traditional probation and incarceration (NIC 1990:3). Although no single definition is widely accepted, the concept of intermediate sanctions implies that the sanctioning of offenders in the community will be measurably enhanced. According to McGarry (1990), regardless of the goal of supervision (e.g., punishment, deterrence, incapacitation), reliance on intermediate sanctions will, at least in concept, provide more of it. As she notes, "[this] can mean increased surveillance, tighter controls on movement, more intense treatment for a wider assortment of maladies or deficiencies, increased offender accountability, and greater emphasis on payments to victims and/or corrections authorities."

Reliance on intermediate sanctions as part of an agency's violations policy may contribute to a more effective system of supervision case management. Where prison and jail crowding is serious, the development of intermediate sanctions may serve to restore credibility to supervision and, at the same time, contribute to the rational and cost-effective management of limited correctional resources.

With respect to parole, when the parole board establishes the conditions governing supervision it is prescribing the goals it expects to be achieved (e.g., risk management, treatment) subsequent to the offender's release. The responsibility for achieving these goals resides with parole field services. If the board's goal is not clear to the field services agency or if the board refers inappropriate candidates, the program's effectiveness will be compromised and the integrity of supervision undermined. The same reasoning applies at the time a judge imposes a term of probation.

For example, a judge or the parole board may place less serious but chronic violators in an intensive supervision program with the understanding that they will be closely monitored. If, however, the program is understood by field staff to be for those who have a serious substance abuse problem and are facing revocation, confusion and uncertainty will quickly develop over its purpose. Under these circumstances, unless the program's purpose is resolved and disseminated to field staff, the rational and effective use of this particular intermediate sanction will be lost.

It is essential that judges, parole boards, and agency decision makers responsible for supervision ensure that field staff understand the fit between responses to violations and the appropriate use of intermediate sanctions.

Intermediate Sanctions Are Not Cost-free

Intermediate sanctions are often perceived to cost less than incarceration. In the long run, this may be so. Yet the initial cost of developing and implementing a range of intermediate sanctions may be significant. Budgetary support and new staff will be required. Even after intermediate sanctions are in place and operational, they will still represent a cost to the agency. If the sanctions are to be meaningful and probation and parole supervision are to have integrity, in most instances, the field services agency must receive additional funding to accomplish its expanded role.

Many community supervision agencies have grown sophisticated in their monitoring and program techniques even though few additional resources have been appropriated. Yet officer workloads must be kept at a manageable level to provide for public safety. While it is easy to observe crowding in prisons, the consequences of caseload crowding is generally not visible in community supervision. Lack of sufficient funding and resources means that most offenders will not receive the programs and services they need to succeed, and the public will not be afforded the surveillance and control it demands.

The use of intermediate sanctions promotes the safety of the community in a cost-effective manner. For example, in Missouri the cost of correctional care in 1991 ranged from $33.71 per day for maximum security custody to $0.05 per day for minimum supervision in the community (Missouri Department of Corrections 1992). At $22.95 per day the department's least costly institutional program is twice that of electronic monitoring, the department's most expensive community-based option, at $11.53 per day.

Some probation and parole agencies have agreed to take on expanded roles without objectively addressing the need for increased agency resources. These agencies are often so pleased to be included as an important player in solving a system-wide problem that they do not want to jeopardize their newly found position by projecting what real costs they will incur or what traditional functions will need to go unattended to succeed with the new program. In many instances agencies have found more efficient ways to operate. Yet there are limits to even improved management efficiency. For example, if small specialized caseloads are newly required but additional staff are not provided, existing caseloads must increase in size. The larger caseloads result in less attention and surveillance per probationer or parolee on regular caseloads, thus compromising the effectiveness of traditional supervision.

An established intermediate sanctions program may be cost-effective for the corrections system as a whole, but start-up costs may be appreciable. To properly administer the program, the budget of the field services agency must be increased. To expect expanded services from the probation and parole agency without the addition of commensurate resources is unreasonable. The ultimate consequence is likely to be a further loss of system credibility or increased failures from the "less supervised" group and more returns to costly prison space.

Supporting Violations Policy with Objective Data

It is not uncommon for legitimate requests by institutional administrators to go unattended until there is a major escape or prison riot, and then both resources and attention are directed toward the crisis. The same is often true for community supervision agencies, although the incident usually involves an offender under supervision who commits a particularly newsworthy offense. Agencies are scrutinized because of the exceptional violator, and restrictive new policies and programs are often imposed on the agency in response to the single exceptional case that is unlikely to reoccur with any frequency.

Another situation sometimes arises that is equally troublesome to agency management. Influential officials, such as senators, commissioners, or judges, attend a conference or become aware of "the greatest" new program or technology. They are eager to fund the new approach, and they want it in operation "by tomorrow." The innovation may not serve the agency policy or a particular offender population well at all, but it would be politically ill-advised for the agency to oppose it. The innovation is funded, and the agency is compelled to ensure successful implementation at any cost.

Developing violation policy as an overreaction to an exceptional case or rushing to implement a program or technology that intrigues someone else is likely to produce failure because exceptional and external conditions would be driving the way in which virtually all cases will be handled by the agency for the foreseeable future. If the exceptional case involved a known violent offender, the policy thus adopted would not affect nonviolent probationers or parolees. If electronic monitoring is funded, it should be used for a carefully defined target population and not for low-risk offenders in the hopes of avoiding newsworthy failures. The enhanced policy or technological surveillance represented by these examples could lead to detected violations by a portion of the offender population that does not present a real problem in the first place. However, because of the attention focused on the agency, there may be a temptation to get tough and revoke anyone who does not fully comply with the conditions of supervision.

All too often field service agencies do not have a command of the data to present informed answers when questions are raised by the media, politicians, or others. This makes the outsider appear to be as much an "expert" as agency administrators, and decisions or pressures may be generated that conflict with the agency's violations policy. If there is a clearly defined policy and approach to dealing with specific types of violation behavior, and if there are objective data to support the wisdom of existing policy, then the agency is in a better position to benefit from the attention it receives.

Reliable and objective data can be used to develop and amend agency policy on an ongoing basis. In recent years the growth of knowledge and technology has resulted in the use of instruments that assist agencies in making offender-based decisions, as well as defensible policy choices. Tools such as risk and needs instruments help to predict offender behavior, and classification and workload instruments aid in the effective deployment of limited resources. Data-based programs for offenders permit the tracking and study of offender performance. The ongoing assessment of this information allows administrators and policy makers to determine what risk certain types of offenders present under supervision. Such information may also be used to project the effect of proposed policy changes, in addition to determining the most effective allocation of agency resources.

Community supervision administrators dread the specter of the "one bad case," and no area is more devastated by a controversial case than violation and revocation practices. Developing and revising such policy through the use of reliable and objective data reduces the likelihood that these cases will occur, and when they do, the agency is equipped to explain how its policies were developed, its rationale, and the effect of any changes proposed thereafter. Likewise, when a particular intermediate sanction is being promoted, the agency can objectively plan for what population it could be used on and forecast what would be its likely affect on current violations practices.

Intermediate Sanctions: Just and Humane

Given long-term budgetary and resource limitations, practitioners must become more sophisticated and purposeful when responding to offender violations, especially the technical violations of supervision that do not involve a crime. It is important to recognize that developing policy regarding technical violations is important to the effective management of probation and parole agencies. It is equally important to acknowledge that the appropriate use of intermediate sanctions as part of an agency's violations policy is also just and humane. While this is perhaps implicit in sound policy, the current interest in intermediate sanctions is driven mainly by prison crowding and tight budgetary constraints. It is not premised on a belief that the use of community-based responses to violations is the right thing to do in and of itself.

In a hypothetical world lacking prison crowding or economic concerns, it would still be appropriate to use intermediate responses for many violators because it is the humane thing to do. Community-based responses should not be viewed as alternatives, but rather prison should be viewed as the alternative to continued community supervision and the responsible use of intermediate sanctions. Currently, three out of every four offenders in the United States are under supervision in the community rather than in jail or in prison.

To some, the words "just" and "humane" conjure an image of purity and wisdom. However, on a more practical level, the issue involves fashioning responses that are fitting and deserved for the act committed. These responses should demonstrate compassion and empathy for human beings who are also offenders. Except for killing or injuring another, our society knows of no more onerous an action than restricting one's liberty through confinement. The effect of this sanction is felt not only by offenders, but also by their families and the public that must pay for their incarceration. This is not to say that no technical violation, or combination of technical violations, merits revocation and return to custody; rather, it is to propose the judicious use of confinement in only those instances where it is specifically mandated given the circumstances of the case. It should be no more than a final alternative.

A predictable reaction to any proposal to change current practices is that it is the job of probation and parole to protect the public and that it is not proper to keep offenders in the community if they do not adhere to conditions of supervision. However, there are different levels of risk presented by offenders, and technical violations in and of themselves seldom present a threat to others. In these instances "system credibility" is primarily at stake. Violations of technical conditions may also be an indication that more serious problems exist in a case. Many times the public is really no safer when a probationer or parolee is revoked, especially if the parole board is forced to release a more serious offender to make room. It is necessary to take some action with technical violators without necessarily returning them to confinement.

With respect to what is just and humane, it is necessary to look as well at the families and others who are affected by how the system responds to technical violations. It is unwise to interrupt an offender's current and viable employment situation because one of the primary goals of community supervision is to encourage the probationer or parolee to be law-abiding and self-sufficient in the community. Whether it involves revocation or detention while processing allegations, removal from the community not only jeopardizes the offender's continued employment, it also carries unintended and often negative consequence for spouses, children, and others.

Public Support for Intermediate Sanctions

Many believe that when an offender commits a crime or violates the conditions of supervision, a term of confinement necessarily and appropriately follows. Were this perception accurate, three out of every four offenders would not already be on probation or parole. It is easy to respond in a survey that all offenders should be incarcerated, but such a view is often softened when the respondent is confronted with specific information about sanctioning options. When informed of the various community-based options that are available there is a surprising amount of public support for the use of intermediate sanctions for certain types of offenders and violations.

A 1989 public opinion study conducted by the Public Agenda Foundation, on behalf of the Clark Foundation, asked Alabama citizens to decide between prison or probation for a number of individual cases. Survey participants were then informed about community-based alternatives and asked to determine the appropriate punishment for each of the cases a second time. The vast majority of those who initially said prison was the appropriate disposition subsequently preferred one of the alternatives. A small number opted for prison over community-based sanctions if the crime involved violence.

Public opinion was surveyed in Delaware in 1991 using the same techniques. The results were remarkably consistent with the Alabama results. Survey participants originally wanted to incarcerate seventeen of twenty-three offenders but reduced that number to five of the twenty-three once they learned about community-based sanctions.

Most technical violations are nonviolent by definition. The International Association on Residential and Community Alternatives sponsored a national survey in September 1991 to assess public attitudes about nondangerous offenders (IARCA 1992). Its findings revealed that 80 percent of the respondents (35 percent strongly, 45 percent somewhat) favored nonprison programs for nondangerous offenders if they are required to hold a job, perform community service, repay their victims, and receive counseling. According to the survey, only one in five indicated that nonviolent criminals belong in prison or that community programs pose a risk.

These studies support the experience of many in probation and parole with respect to technical violations. The public supports efforts to manage the offender population in the community in a reasonable manner. It does not expect every offender to be returned to custody for minor technical violations, although it is very concerned abut violent behavior. Although the public does not want offenders to remain under community supervision when their behavior represents a threat to the public or when the offender chronically ignores conditions of supervision, neither is there a significant demand for removal of technical violators from supervision.

The lesson gained from the Alabama and Delaware sentencing studies is that with accurate information the public solidly supports nonprison sanctions for nonviolent offenders. It is the task of the probation and parole administrators to provide timely information to the public and others in the justice system so that they may recognize that intermediate sanctions, if properly developed, represent the most appropriate response to many violations by those under community supervision.

References

Bureau of Justice Statistics. 1991. *Probation and parole 1990.* Washington, D.C.: U.S. Department of Justice.

Bureau of Justice Statistics. 1984. *Returning to prison.* Washington, D.C.: U.S. Department of Justice.

Burke, P. B., et al. 1990. *The National Institute of Corrections model case management and classification project: A case study in diffusion.* Washington, D.C.: National Institute of Corrections.

Herrick, E. 1989. Parole revocation. *Corrections Compendium* (March): 8-9.

McGarry, P. 1990. Intermediate sanctions. *Community Corrections Quarterly* 1 (Spring): 1-6.

Missouri Department of Corrections. 1992. *Continuum of service.* Jefferson City, Mo.: Missouri Department of Corrections.

Public Agenda Foundation. 1989. *Punishing criminals—The public's view.* New York: Edna McConnell Clark Foundation.

Public Agenda Foundation. 1991. *Punishing criminals—The people of Delaware consider the options.* New York: Edna McConnell Clark Foundation.

Wirthlin Group. 1992. *IARCA survey.* LaCrosse, Wis.: International Association on Residential and Community Alternatives.

About the Authors

L. Russell "Rusty" Burress has been on the staff of the U.S. Sentencing Commission in Washington, D.C., since it was established in 1985. He is involved in the training of judges, probation officers, and attorneys in the use of sentencing guidelines.

Burress has been a probation officer since 1976, serving for nine years in the District of South Carolina and the past seven years on detail to the U.S. Sentencing Commission. He was appointed principal training advisor to the commission in May 1992.

He has a bachelor's degree from the University of South Carolina in Columbia and a master's degree in probation and parole studies from Fordham University.

Jasper R. Clay, Jr., was appointed to the U.S. Parole Commission in 1984; he was appointed vice-chair of the commission in 1991.

In 1958, he served as a parole and probation agent, a position he held until 1966 when he became a staff training and development specialist. From 1969 to 1984, Clay served on the Maryland State Parole Board (now the Maryland Parole Commission).

Clay has a B.S. degree from Morgan State University in psychology. He is a member of the American Correctional Association and has served on the board of directors of Threshold Halfway House and as Middle Atlantic representative on the executive board of the Association of Paroling Authorities.

Jude Del Preore has served as the vicinage chief probation officer for both Morris and Sussex counties, New Jersey, since 1989.

He is a certified trainer and serves on the adjunct faculty of Seton Hall Law School, two county colleges, the New Jersey State Police Academy, several county police academies, and the New Jersey State Administrative Office of the Courts Training and Development Unit.

Del Preore completed his undergraduate and graduate education in public administration at Rutgers University. He is certified as a fellow of the Institute of Court Management. Del Preore is an active member of several professional organizations, including the American Correctional Association and the American Probation and Parole Association.

Henry R. Grinner, Jr., is director of program development for the U.S. Parole Commission in Chevy Chase, Maryland. He has served the Parole Commission since 1974 as a hearing examiner and as a regional administrator.

Grinner has a bachelor's degree in political science and sociology from Tennessee University and a master's degree in correctional administration (criminology) from Xavier University. He is a member of the American Correctional Association, the Association of Paroling Authorities International, the American Probation and Parole Association, and the National Council on Crime and Delinquency.

John Grubbs has been the deputy commissioner of Community Services in the Mississippi Department of Corrections since 1985. He served the Mississippi

Department of Youth Services from 1970 to 1980. He left his position as assistant superintendent there to join the Mississippi Department of Corrections.

Grubbs has a bachelor's degree in psychology from the University of Southern Mississippi. He is active in the American Correctional Association, the Mississippi Associate of Professionals in Corrections, and the American Probation and Parole Association.

Paul Herman has worked for the Missouri Board of Probation and Parole for over twenty years. He began his career as a probation and parole officer and has held numerous supervisory and management positions in the agency. He has been the chief state supervisor since 1985 and is responsible for the administration of field and institutional probation and parole staff.

Kermit Humphries is a correctional program specialist for the National Institute of Corrections (NIC), where he monitors grant and technical assistance activities for the NIC, Community Corrections Division, in Washington, D.C.

Before joining NIC in 1985, he served as community corrections planner for the Alaska Department of Corrections. During his fourteen years in Alaska, he was an administrator at a private residential facility for delinquent boys and served in a variety of state probation/parole and Department of Corrections central office positions.

Humphries earned his M.A. in sociology from the Fordham University graduate program for probation/parole officers. His B.A. is from Biola University in La Mirada, California.

Ronald W. Jackson is the director of parole for the Georgia State Board of Pardons and Paroles. He served previously as director of Field Operations for the board and as parole commissioner for the Texas State Board of Pardons and Paroles from 1984 to 1990. He has served as manager of Membership Services for the American Correctional Association and as executive director of the Texas Corrections Association. He has worked in several capacities for the Texas Department of Corrections. Jackson was co-chair of the ACA Task Force on Parole. He holds a B.S. in criminal justice from Sam Houston State University.

Jacqueline Marie Klosak is director of program evaluation for the Cook County Adult Probation Department in Chicago, Illinois. Her primary responsibilities include developing and implementing the department's evaluation process, which includes creating program evaluation methodologies, formatting reporting documents, performing the evaluation, and communicating the evaluation results to the appropriate personnel. She is also responsible for initiating and supervising the daily process of quality assurance, providing written documentation of the quality assurance results to appropriate personnel, and directly supervising the quality assurance specialist.

Klosak previously served as a probation officer for the Cook County Adult Probation Department from 1987 to 1989. She has a bachelor's degree in sociology/criminal justice from Valparaiso University and a master's degree in justice administration from the University of Louisville. She is currently a doctoral student in public policy analysis at the University of Illinois.

Arthur J. Lurigio, a social psychologist, is currently an associate professor of criminal justice at Loyola University and director of research for the Cook County, Illinois, Adult Probation Department. He received his doctorate from Loyola University of Chicago in 1984 and has published extensively in several areas. His research interests include community crime prevention, criminal victimization and victim services, intermediate punishments, monetary sanctions, decision making among criminal justice professionals, crime and mental disorders, and AIDS in the criminal justice system.

The New York State Division of Parole's Office of Policy Analysis and Information includes the operational units of quality and control, which is responsible for the daily processing of information and error rectification from statewide parole offices, the parole board, and other criminal justice agencies; management information services, which provides system application, programming, and telecommunications services for the division; and policy analysis, which is responsible for monitoring the performance of the division's programs as well as statistical and policy analysis.

The Policy Analysis Unit designs and authors the division's policy analyses, with regard to information generated within and from outside the agency. The unit is responsible for program monitoring and assessments, as well as population projections of board and operational functions, and reviews of important criminal justice developments for management decision makers.

Don Page is the regional director for the Western region of the Ministry of Correctional Services for the Province of Ontario. He is stationed in London, Ontario. A thirty-year veteran of corrections, Page has worked as a probation and parole officer, a probation manager, a correctional officer, an institutional superintendent, and a corrections executive. He is active in many correctional organizations and is currently a member of the Board of Governors of the American Correctional Association. He is a past director and a charter member of the American Probation and Parole Association.

Dale G. Parent joined Abt Associates, a research firm in Cambridge, Massachusetts, as a senior analyst in law and public safety in 1987. At Abt he has conducted studies on boot camp prison programs, day reporting centers, offender fee payments, and crime victim compensation programs for the National Institute of Justice (NIJ). Currently he is directing an NIJ study of state practices to structure probation and parole revocations and to apprehend and punish absconders. He also is directing a national assessment of conditions of confinement in secure juvenile facilities for the Office of Juvenile Justice and Delinquency Prevention.

From 1982 to 1987, Parent served as deputy director of the National Institute for Sentencing Alternatives at Brandeis University. During the 1982-83 academic year, he was a Guggenheim Fellow at the Yale Law School. From 1978 to 1982, he directed Minnesota's Sentencing Guidelines Commission. In 1974, he joined the research staff of the Minnesota Department of Corrections. From 1968 to 1972, he was a corrections planner for the Governor's Commission on Crime Prevention and Control, in St. Paul, Minnesota.

John P. Prevost is the assistant director of special parole services for the Georgia State Board of Pardons and Paroles. He coordinates the planning and development of new programs that support the agency's field staff. He has worked as both a line parole officer and field manager for the parole board.

He received his bachelor's degree in biology from Saint Meinrad College and his master's degree in public administration from Georgia State University.

Edward E. Rhine is the deputy director of field services for the Georgia State Board of Pardons and Paroles. He previously served as the assistant chief in the Probation Services Division, Administrative Office of the Courts, Trenton, New Jersey; executive assistant to the chairman of the New Jersey State Parole Board; and accreditation manager for the New Jersey Department of Corrections. He served as co-chair of the ACA Task Force on Parole. He is co-editor of *Observations on Parole: A Collection of Readings from Western Europe, Canada and the United States* (1987) and *Correction Theory and Practice*. He also recently coauthored *Paroling Authorities: Recent History and Current Practice* (ACA 1991).

He received his B.A. in sociology from Ohio University and his M.A. and Ph.D., also in sociology, from Rutgers University.

John J. Robinson was appointed undersheriff of Cook County in 1991. Prior to his appointment as undersheriff, Robinson served as the chief probation officer of the Cook County Adult Probation Department, a position he had held since 1988.

Robinson currently serves as an adjunct faculty member in criminal justice at Chicago State University. He has a B.A. degree from Carroll College, an M.S. degree from State University of New York at Albany, a C.A.S. from Syracuse University, and a J.D. from Northern Illinois University. He is a member of the Illinois Bar.

Lloyd G. Rupp has recently been appointed commissioner of the Alaska Department of Corrections. He previously served as director of corrections at the U.S. Naval Consolidated Brig in Charleston, South Carolina. Rupp holds a bachelor's degree in political science from Fresno State University, a bachelor's and a master's degree from the Church Divinity School of the Pacific, a master's degree in law enforcement from Columbia Pacific University, a doctorate in theology from the San Francisco Theological Seminary, and doctorate in psychology from Columbia Pacific University.

Richard P. Stroker is deputy commissioner of the South Carolina Department of Probation, Parole, and Pardon Services. Stroker received a B.S. degree from Cornell University in 1975 and a J.D. degree from the University of South Carolina in 1978. He worked as a staff attorney and as the executive assistant to the commissioner for Legal Settlements and Compliance for the South Carolina Department of Corrections before coming to the South Carolina Department of Probation, Parole, and Pardon Services as chief legal counsel in 1986. He was promoted to his current position in 1987. Stroker serves as an adjunct professor to the University of South Carolina's College of Criminal Justice.